The Elemental Magic Workbook

For my brothers and sisters
who know there may be no absolute truths,
will to dance in the crawling chaos,
dare to practice the art and science of magic,
and keep silent with our secrets.

The Elemental Magic Workbook

An Experimental Guide to Understanding and Working with the Classical Elements

Soror Velchanes

Megalithica Books
Stafford England

The Elemental Magic Workbook: An Experimental Guide
to Understanding and Working with the Classical Elements
by Soror Velchanes
© 2018 First edition

Cover Design: Storm Constantine/Danielle Lainton
Editor: Megan Besner
Interior Layout: Storm Constantine

Set in Book Antiqua

MB0197
ISBN: 978-1-912241-05-7

A Megalithica Books Publication
http://www.immanion-press.com
info@immanion-press.com

Contents

Legal Notes

This workbook is for entertainment purposes only. It is not a substitute for medical, legal, or financial counsel. The author and publisher assume no legal liability for damages, losses, or other consequences of reader decisions subsequent to, or based on, the contents and activities presented herein.

Introduction

Elemental magic is a living, evolving tradition. Since its inception, individuals from a diversity of backgrounds and preparations have used the elements for spiritual enrichment, life balance, practical magic, and more. Though many cultures developed similar (and also valuable) models, our primary emphasis will be on understanding and working with the elements from classical Greek and Hermetic perspectives, with a chaos magic twist. Different aspects of the universe may be influenced through the forces underlying each element. Here you will explore the nature of each element, how it impacts your life, and how you may harness it for personal benefit.

This workbook has been optimized for self-study. The benefits you will reap will be in direct proportion to your efforts. Chapters should be viewed in sequential order, as latter ones build on previous concepts. A typical chapter is divided into lecture (note-taking) and practice sections. The content covered in a lecture will be reinforced in practice. After exploring how each element impacts your life you will perform magical work tailored to each element. This includes attuning, entrance, invoking, and banishing rites. Elemental monasticisms are also provided.

You should progress at a rate of no more than one chapter per month. The note-taking for a chapter should take no more than two hours to complete, and may be done in one sitting. Magical practice should be commenced for a minimum of 30 minutes each day for the remainder of the month. Take your time and do not rush.

It is highly recommended that you document your efforts in a magical diary to keep track of information and monitor your progress. A magical diary serves as a permanent, written record of your work. It is a place to record your rites, results, insights, and more. Your diary does not have to be fancy unless you want it to be. A cheap spiral-bound notebook or a bound composition notebook should suffice.

Chapter 1
Getting Started

Congratulations on beginning your elemental journey! Throughout history individuals from a diverse variety of backgrounds and preparations have used the elements as means to different ends. In modern times these ends primarily involve spiritual enrichment, life balance, and practical magic. Working with the elements is a highly personal experience. Your perception, internalization, and interaction with each element may be different from your peers, even if you share similar personalities or worldviews.

Greek Model of the Elements

The first recorded mention of the four "roots" comprising all matter is attributed to the Presocratic philosopher Empedocles. Though other Presocratics suggested the "original stuff" composing material existence is water (Thales in Aristotle, *Met.* 1.3, 983b6-27 = DK 11A12, trans. 2001), air (Anaximenes in Theophrastus, quoted by Simplicius, 24.26-25.1 = DK 13A5, trans. 2011), earth (Xenophanes in Hippolytus, 1.14.3-6 = DK 21A33, trans. 2011), or fire (Heraclitus in Plutarch, 338d-e = DK 22B90, trans. 2011), it was Empedocles who proposed these four "roots" existed together in various combinations (in Aëtius, 1.3.20 = DK 31B6, trans. 2011), mixed by the motive forces of love and strife (in Simplicius, 158.1-159.4 [lines 1-35] + Strasbourg Papyrus *ensemble* a [lines 26-69] = DK 31B17 + Strasbourg Papyrus, *ensemble* a , trans. 2011). In his hexameter poetry Empedocles writes, "Hear first the four roots of all things: Shining Zeus and life-bringing Hera and Aidoneus and Nestis, who with her tears gives moisture to the source of mortals" (Aëtius, 1.3.20 = DK 31B6, trans. 2011). Zeus is attributed to air, Hera to earth, Aidoneus (Hades) to fire, and Nestis (Persephone) to water.

While Plato appears to have first called them "elements" (Gk. στοιχεῖα; *Timaeus*, 48a), it was Aristotle who popularized the notion that the classical elements are matter with certain qualities and may be differentiated by their hot/cold and wet/dry characteristics (*Gen. et Corr.* 2.3, 330a30-b7, trans. 2001). The elements have unique combinations of qualities and coexist in various ratios to form material existence (Figure 1.1). The elements may interact with each other, and one element may transform into another if its hot/cold and wet/dry qualities are manipulated (1.1, 314b15–27; 2.1, 329a35–b3; 2.4). In addition, Aristotle integrated Plato's aether (*Timaeus*, 58d) as the quintessence, or fifth element (*DC* 1.3, 270b20-26, trans. 2001). In contrast to the other elements aether lacks hot/cold and wet/dry characteristics, and is fixed and unchanging. The Aristotelian model evolved and perpetuated for almost two millennia, inspiring western spirituality, philosophy, medicine, psychology, and more.

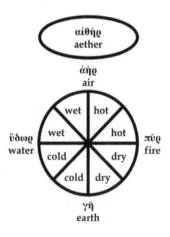

Figure 1.1. Greek model of the elements. The terrestrial elements are differentiated by their hot/cold and wet/dry characteristics. Earth is cold and dry, air is hot and wet, water is cold and wet, and fire is hot and dry. Aether transcends hot/cold and wet/dry characteristics. The ancient Greek word for each element is shown above its English counterpart.

Hermetic Model of the Elements

The earliest recorded mention of the elements in the Hermetic tradition appears in *Poimandres* of the *Corpus Hermeticum* (Copenhaver (Trans.), 1995). This collection of texts is attributed to the "Thrice Great" Hermes Trismegistus, a combination of the Greek Hermes and Egyptian Thoth. In a vision of the universe's creation, fire manifests from light, followed by air, with the water and earth elements remaining mixed below (I.5, trans. 1995). The upward moving elements (fire and air) are creative, whereas the downward moving elements (water and earth) are nourishing (*Ascl.* II, trans. 1995). In a second emanation, seven "governors" (classical planets) ruling fate are created from the upward moving elements (I.9, trans. 1995). The *logos* then rises from the downward moving elements, ultimately setting the planets into orbit (I.10-11, trans. 1995).

Bardon (trans. 1956/2001) further explains how the elements manifested from aether. The aether is unknowable, indefinable primal energy, the "All in All" which many paradigms call "God" (p. 30). The first element to manifest was fire, characterized by heat and expansion (the electric principle). Its opposite element is water, which is cold and contractive (the magnetic principle). Together these opposite principles form everything in the universe (Figure 1.2). The air element emerged to mediate between fire and water. Earth was the last element to manifest and gives the others a concrete form.

Our bodies are a mixture of the four elements and their unique combination within us influences our personality (Bardon, trans. 1956/2001). This is reflected in the four humors doctrine developed by Hippocratic authors (see Page et al. (Eds.), trans. 1931/1959a; trans. 1931/1959b) and expanded by Galen (cited in Arikha, 2007). In this model the humors (body fluids) are the bearers of elemental properties in the human body. They are responsible for our health and personality, and their imbalance causes disease and discontentment. The four humors doctrine spread from ancient Greece and dominated western thinking until the 1800s. It is still present in alternative medical traditions and many forms of folk medicine today.

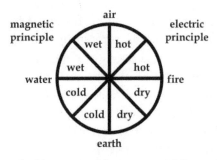

Figure 1.2. The Hermetic tetrapolar magnet. The center of the circle where all four characteristics meet is the depth point/aether. To make a colored image for your notes traditional correspondences are as follows – electric principle, red; magnetic principle, blue; earth, brown or black; air, sky blue; water, blue-green; and fire, red (Bardon, trans. 1956/2001). For the principles color the right half of the page outside of the circle red, and the left half of the page outside of the circle blue. For the elements color in the bottom two triangles inside the circle for earth, the top two triangles for air, the left two triangles for water, and the right two triangles for fire.

The *Qabala*

The *Qabala* [Heb. קבלה] is a cornerstone of the western esoteric tradition. It is a way of reception (of the nature of the universe) and revelation. Its wisdom can be summarized into one glyph: the *Tree of Life* (Figure 1.3).

The *Tree of Life* is a map of the self, all levels of experience, and the universe. It is composed of 10 spheres and 22 paths. A complete *Tree of Life* exists in four worlds, which we will explore more deeply in later chapters. Each world represents a different aspect of the unfolding of creation and corresponds to a particular element as well as a letter of the Tetragrammaton [Heb. יהוה], the proper four-letter name of the God of Israel. One can easily spend a lifetime studying the *Qabala*, and indeed many people do. A detailed discussion of the *Qabala* is beyond the scope of this workbook, but additional information and recommended reading, should you choose to pursue it, are given in Appendix A.

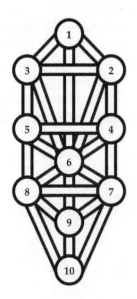

Figure 1.3. The *Qabalistic Tree of Life*. The *Tree of Life* is one of the most widespread symbols in Jewish mysticism. Its spheres and paths represent specific archetypal forces. Romanized Hebrew names of each sphere are as follows – 1, *Keter* [Heb. Crown]; 2, *Ḥakma* [Wisdom]; 3, *Bina* [Understanding]; 4, *Ḥesed* [Love]; 5, *Gebura* [Strength]; 6, *Tif'eret* [Beauty]; 7, *Neṣaḥ* [Victory]; 8, *Hod* [Splendor]; 9, *Yesod* [Foundation]; and 10, *Malkut* [Kingdom].

The Pentagram

The pentagram (five-pointed star) is significant in many cultures. It is a shape that can be drawn unicursally (in a single stroke). The earliest discovered pentagrams date back to the ancient world where they were used in Mesopotamian ideographic writing (Magini, 2015). The symbol eventually spread to other regions. In ancient Greece the *pentalpha* was a sign of recognition among the Pythagoreans and considered a symbol of good health (Schwartzman, 1994; Simonyi, 1978/2012). Early Hebrews associated the pentagram with the five books of the *Tora* (Stein & Stein, 2016). Early Christians associated the pentagram with the five wounds of Christ (Stein & Stein, 2016).

Drawing a pentagram inherently involves working with elemental forces (Figure 1.4). In Renaissance times Agrippa (trans. 1531-1533/2004) viewed the pentagram as a protective symbol capable of commanding evil spirits. In the 1800s, Lévi (trans. 1896/2001) viewed it as a sign of intellectual omnipotence, autocracy, and the microcosm. Lévi writes the pentagram "...signifies the domination of the mind over the elements, and the demons of air, the spirits of fire, the phantoms of water and ghosts of earth are enchained by this sign" (p. 63). In many western esoteric traditions today, the pentagram continues to symbolize protection, balance, and man as a microcosm.

ש
aether

א air — water ה

earth   fire

ה [final]   י

Figure 1.4. The pentagram. Each pentagram point corresponds to an element and a letter of the Pentagrammaton (Crowley, 1909/1999). The Pentagrammaton [Heb. יהשוה; YHShWH] is the five-letter reconstructed name of Jesus.

Study Tips

1. Make sure your environment is conducive to learning. A private, quiet place free of distractions is ideal.
2. Develop a routine. Establish a set schedule where you work on a chapter at the same time each day.
3. Performing magic in the same locale over a long enough time period will eventually cause an automatic shift in your consciousness when you enter, so a consistent location is also helpful.
4. Take your time and do not rush. Move on to the next chapter when you have a firm grasp on content in the current chapter.

5. Though the elements coexist together in a balanced fashion it is easiest to focus on one element at a time in the beginning.
6. Learning magic is a lot like learning math. Proficiency is gained through experience. You have to do many math problems (or many magical rites) to get good at it.

Creating and Maintaining a Magical Diary

A magical diary serves as a permanent, written record of your work. Your diary does not have to be fancy unless you want it to be. A cheap spiral-bound notebook or a bound composition notebook should suffice. Do not let anyone view your magical diary – it is a highly personal document for you alone. Also, do not touch someone else's diary or other magical items without their permission – it is considered rude. Instructions for creating a basic magical diary are as follows:

1. Create a Table of Contents to record a page number, date, and title for each entry. Leaving a small space to mark if a rite yielded successful results is helpful but is not required.
2. Individual entries should begin with the date and title. Additional information (e.g. time, moon phase, weather…) may also be included if it is important in your tradition or if you feel it is necessary.
3. Include a brief description of what you did. Elaborate workings may be referenced or copied in their entirety into the diary. Securely attaching printouts by stapling or taping is another option.
4. Record any notes, thoughts, feelings, and other details you feel are important afterwards. Document them as soon as possible so you don't forget small details.

5. Leave a few blank lines to record any results (or lack thereof) you achieve. The manifestation of results varies widely and depends on factors such as the overarching goal and nature of the activity.

An example magical diary entry is shown below:

17-Sep 2015. 6:30PM MST. Earth Element Meditation. I meditated on the earth element for 10 minutes, barefoot and in the garden. The stress of the day has dissipated away, and I feel calmer and more grounded now. The earth element was thick, heavy, quiet, steady, and silent.

A second, more complex example entry is shown below. Never write anyone's legal name in your diary. Refer to people by their magical names or initials instead. This will protect peoples' identities if your diary is accidentally discovered. Better safe than sorry!

September 24, 2016. 10:16PM MST. Serafim Disco Inferno. I performed the fire element rite stapled on the adjacent page with FE, W, and DS tonight. We finished about an hour ago. The negative trait I chose to "purify" away is my bad temper. I achieved a gnostic state more rapidly than usual and it also came on abnormally strong.

Addendum. October 10, 2016. There have been a few major situations where I did not lose my temper when I otherwise would have. Friends and coworkers also recently commented that I seem less angry lately. In addition to the rite, I've made a concerted effort to make life in general as calm as possible.

Keep your diary in a safe, secure place where no one will see it. Update it regularly to keep track of your progress. It is not uncommon for long-term practitioners to have multiple volumes. Sometimes it is fun to look back and see what you were doing years ago! If you already have a magical diary begin a separate one for your elemental work. Important entries can be referenced or copied into the primary diary.

How to Meditate

Though many meditation techniques exist their overarching goal is to focus your energy inward to carefully examine a subject of interest – its underlying forces can be more easily perceived by the subconscious mind. The procedure below can be used to meditate on any topic. Feel free to print out these instructions and display them in your study area.

1. Sit down in a comfortable position in a quiet place free of distractions.
2. Close your eyes.
3. Focus your attention on your breath but make no effort to control the intensity or rhythm of your breathing.
4. If your mind wanders gently redirect your focus back to your breathing.
5. After a few minutes transfer your focus from breathing to the subject of interest.
6. If your mind wanders gently redirect your focus back to the subject of interest.
7. When you are finished open your eyes and take a moment to become reacquainted with your surroundings. Once you are reoriented you may stand up.
8. Record your results in your magical diary.
9. In the beginning you may skip Steps 5-6 and just focus on your breath. During this exercise you might also observe peripheral thoughts entering and exiting your mind. Let them go and do not pursue them.

Chapter 1 Homework

After taking notes on the chapter proceed with the following exercises. Magical practice should be commenced for a minimum of 30 minutes each day for the remainder of the month.

1. Obtain and keep a magical diary for a minimum of one month. If you already have a magical diary begin a separate one for your elemental work.
2. Practice meditating on any topic for 20 minutes each day for a minimum of one month. You may choose two 10-minute sessions or one 20-minute session. Record your results in your magical diary.
3. Reflect on what you hope to gain from working with the elements for your remaining 10 minutes each day. How do the elements impact your life? How do they impact the world around you? Record your thoughts and feelings in your magical diary.

Fire burns, water churns, air carries, earth buries.
–My Grandfather

I remember my grandfather saying this when I was a child. He taught me much of what I know about the *Qabala* and was a catalyst to my interest in magic. I am unsure whether this is his original saying or if he heard it somewhere else. Now I pass it on to you.

Chapter 2
Earth Buries

Earth provides the foundation and stability necessary to work with the elements, thus our journey will begin with earth. The alchemical and *tattva* symbols for the earth element are shown in Figure 2.1. They are useful focal points in meditation and magical practice.

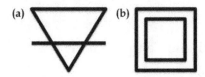

Figure 2.1. Common earth element symbols. The (a) alchemical and (b) westernized *tattva* for elemental earth are shown. The *tattvas* are Hindu in origin but are occasionally used in western traditions. To make a colored image for your notes color the *tattva* (inner square) yellow and its background (larger square) dark purple.

The Western View of Earth

In the Greek model earth is cold and dry (Aristotle, *Gen. et Corr.* 2.3, 330a30-b7, trans. 2001). The hot quality brings together similar things, whereas the cold quality brings together all things, regardless of their similarity (2.2, 329b25-31). Elements that are wet are adaptable in shape, whereas dry elements are not (2.2, 329b31-33). Hippocratic authors write that earth manifests in black bile, the retentive humor (Page et al. (Eds.), trans. 1931/1959a). Each humor is associated with a particular season of the year and age range, during which an excess of the humor may be present in the body. Black bile predominates in autumn and in those of mature (25-45 years old) age (trans.

1931/1959a). The Roman physician Galen attributed a preponderance of this fluid to the melancholic temperament (cited in Arikha, 2007).

The Hermetic model expands on the Greek model, though some differences exist. In the Hermetic view earth is not considered a "true" element – it is a product of interactions between air, water, and fire (Bardon, trans. 1956/2001). Earth contains the other three elements and gives them a solid, concrete form. It is the densest element, and its existence allows for the physical manifestation of creation. Psychologically, elemental earth reigns over our self-preservation and propagation instincts (Bardon, trans. 1956/2001).

The Melancholic Temperament

The four Galenic temperaments (melancholic, sanguine, phlegmatic, and choleric) are key concepts in ancient Greek and Hermetic thought. Each temperament is characterized by distinct personality traits. The melancholic is inclined towards introspection, the sanguine towards optimism, the phlegmatic towards sluggishness, and the choleric towards a quick temper (discussed in Arikha, 2007). Categorizing the key traits of each temperament as introvert/extrovert and emotionally stable/unstable, as given in Eysenck's *Dimensions of Personality* (1947/1998), results in groupings reflective of Galen-Kant-Wundt descriptions of people (see Miles & Hempel, 2004).

The preponderance of black bile in the melancholic predisposes them towards an introspective, thoughtful personality, but also towards delirium and symptoms associated with modern day depression (Arikha, 2007). Melancholics are also susceptible to hypochondriac diseases (Arikha, 2007). See Table 2.1 for a partial list of traits traditionally associated with the melancholic temperament.

Table 2.1. *The Melancholic Temperament*

Eysenck Traits[a]	Hermetic Virtues[b]	Hermetic Vices[b]
Moody	Respectful	Stubborn
Anxious	Persevering	Obstinate
Rigid	Conscientious	Easily offended
Sober	Thorough	Lazy
Pessimistic	Punctual	Ponderous
Reserved	Responsible	Uncompromising
Unsociable	Prudent	Melancholic
Quiet	Cautious	Slow-moving

[a]Eysenck traits are adapted from *Dimensions of Personality* (Eysenck, 1947/1998). [b]Hermetic traits are adapted from *Initiation into Hermetics* (Bardon, trans. 1956/2001).

Western Earth Magic

In many western esoteric traditions earth is associated with nature, growth, fertility, prosperity, wealth, stability, binding, and birth/death magic. In witchcraft its cardinal direction is north, its time is midnight, and its season is winter (Starhawk, 1979/1999). Our sense of touch and the colors brown and green are also associated with elemental earth (Starhawk, 1979/1999). Further, in witchcraft each elemental force is represented by a tool. The earth element is represented by the pentacle (Starhawk, 1979/1999).

There are four virtues said to be essential to magic. They are the Four Powers of the Sphinx: to know, to will, to dare, and to keep silent (Lévi, trans. 1896/2001). The virtue associated with elemental earth is "to keep silent" (Crowley, 1909/1999). Deities traditionally associated with elemental earth include Nephthys (Egyptian), Demeter (Greek), Ceres (Roman), and Prithivi (Hindu).

In ceremonial traditions the earth element [Heb. ארץ; *areṣ*] is associated with the *Qabalistic* path connecting *Yesod* [Foundation] and *Malkut* [Kingdom] (Crowley, 1909/1999). It is also associated with *'Asiya*, the "Material World" (Crowley, 1909/1999). This is the world of manifestation, matter, and interaction between our body and the external world (Parfitt, 1991). It is the final ה of the Tetragrammaton, the completion of form. Earth is feminine, receptive, passive, solid, slow moving, and physical. Its *Qabalistic* King scale colors are *Malkut's* citrine, olive, russet, and black, which represent elemental air, water, fire, and earth, respectively (Crowley, 1909/1999). Its traditional ceremonial tool is the pentacle (Crowley, 1909/1999). The "top-down" Hebrew hierarchy, sans demons, for elemental earth is shown in Table 2.2.

Table 2.2. *The Earth Element Ceremonial Hierarchy*

Qabalistic World	Level	Name
אצילות ['Aṣilut]	Divine name	אדני ['Adonay][a]
בריאה [Beri 'a]	Archangel	אוריאל ['Uri 'el]
יצירה [Yeṣirah]	Angelic choirs[b]	כרובים [Kerubim]
	Angel[c]	פורלאך [Forlak]
	Elemental king[d]	Gob
	Elementals[e]	Gnomes
עשיה ['Asiya]	Magical tool	Pentacle[f]

Information is adapted from *777 Revised* (Crowley, 1909/1999). Romanized Hebrew names are in brackets. See Appendix B for pronunciations, etymologies, and more. [a] *'Adonay Ha 'areṣ* is "(my) Lord of the Earth" in *Malkut*. [b]Singular choirs are called the "elemental ruler" in many occult texts. [c]The elemental angel names are written on the Seventh Pentacle of the Sun in *The Key of Solomon the King* (Mathers (Ed.), trans. 1889/2009). [d]Lévi never states the source language of the elemental king names in *Transcendental Magic: Its Doctrine and Ritual* (trans. 1896/2001). [e]Paracelsus describes the elementals in *Liber de Nymphis* (trans. 1941/1996). [f]Salt in some traditions.

The Four *Qabalistic* Worlds

The four *Qabalistic* worlds represent different levels of the heavens and reflect the process of creating the universe. A complete *Tree of Life* is present in all four worlds, with the *Malkut* of one world manifesting the *Keter* of the next. Various denizens occupy these worlds. Magicians may contact them to obtain knowledge, cause internal or external change, and more. They are typically called in a "top-down" fashion to refine the magician's request.

The highest world, 'Aṣilut, is the divine and unchanging "Archetypal World." It consists of pure principles and archetypes (DuQuette, 2001; Fortune, 1935/2000; Kaplan, 1997). Universal qualities and divine names reside here (DuQuette, 2001). Magicians vibrate divine names to resonate with particular aspects of the "All in All" or "God." Each element is associated with a particular divine name.

The second world is Beri'a, the "Creative World." It is the first world created *ex nihilo*, and thus the first separated from the divine (Kaplan (Trans.), 1997). This is where archangels receive concepts and qualities emanated from 'Aṣilut (DuQuette, 2001). Archangels direct the manifestation of creation, and lesser angels and spirits are obedient to them. Each element is associated with a particular archangel.

The third world is Yeṣirah, the "Formative World." This is the world of thoughts and ideas, where specific designs begin to take shape (DuQuette, 2001; Fortune, 1935/2000). Angelic choirs and angels reside here (DuQuette, 2001; Fortune, 1935/2000). The elemental choirs may be called on when you need to obtain information in that element's nature. The elemental angels are personifications of each element. Their names originate from *The Key of Solomon the King*. Together they are the guiding forces behind an elemental king.

Elemental kings and the elementals they command also reside in Yeṣirah (Fortune, 1935/2000; Pepin, 1989). The elemental king represents the collective consciousness of the elementals and is the driving force behind their actions. The elementals facilitate the physical manifestation of an element in 'Asiya. The kings and elementals are the most effective at accomplishing tasks on the material plane, as they are the closest to it. The elemental king names originate from Lévi's *Transcendental Magic: Its Doctrine and Ritual*. The elementals were first described in detail by Paracelsus (see *Liber de Nymphis*). Despite its Latin title the body of the work is in German.

The fourth world is *'Asiya*, the "Material World." This is the world of matter and physical manifestation and is the most tangible and dense of the four worlds (Fortune, 1935/2000; Parfitt, 1991). It consists of our physical world and its spiritual shadow (Fortune, 1935/2000; Kaplan (Trans.), 1997). We live here. Our elemental tools reside here. Other denizens of *'Asiya* include intelligences, spirits, and demons (DuQuette, 2001; Fortune, 1935/2000).

Gnosis

Gnosis is an altered state of consciousness and a key ingredient in magic. Achieving gnosis serves to bypass the conscious mind so our intent may be uploaded into the universe (Carroll, 1987). Methods of reaching gnosis can be broadly classified as "inhibitory" or "excitatory" (p. 33). Inhibitory gnosis involves gradually silencing the mind until a single point of focus remains, while excitatory gnosis involves exciting the mind until it overloads, paralyzing everything but a single point of focus. Chemognosis (gnosis reached by chemical means) is another option (Carroll, 1987; Wetzel, 2001). Though many magicians throughout time have used it effectively, it is risky because the mind may be difficult to control in this state. It will not be addressed in this workbook.

The gnostic state is challenging to describe in words; it must be experienced directly. When you achieve this state you will instinctively know it. Your internal dialogue freezes or disappears entirely. The surrounding environment becomes irrelevant. In that moment a single point of focus is all that exists. The more frequently you reach a gnostic state the easier it becomes to reach again. A partial list of inhibitory and excitatory gnosis methods are listed below. Feel free to come up with your own. The only limit is your imagination!

Inhibitory Gnosis:
Methods of inhibitory gnosis include sleep deprivation, fasting, sensory deprivation (such as blindfolding your eyes or plugging your nose), prolonged gazing or staring (such as into a mirror or crystal), repeating *mantras*, meditation, prolonged motionlessness, and focused visualization.

Excitatory Gnosis:
Methods of excitatory gnosis include pain, exhaustion (such as through dancing or exercising), hyperventilation, strong emotion (such as confronting a fear), sensory overload (such as biting into a hot pepper while listening to loud music), holding your breath for as long as possible, spinning, and glossolalia.

Earth in Chaos Magic

The earth element may be applied to magical practice in numerous ways. Various egregores, godforms, or pop culture characters associated with elemental earth may be invoked or evoked. Divination may be practiced via reading rocks, leaves, or through geomancy. Knot magic may be employed in binding rites. Burying magical tools or other objects in dirt or salt for a few days serves to purify them. Seeds and coins may be planted for fertility and wealth. Images may be created in sand or soil. People may bury or cover themselves in dirt during death/rebirth or metamorphosis rites.

Rites for elemental earth are listed in this chapter. The attunement exercise familiarizes you with the forces underlying each element. The entrance rite formally introduces you to the element and facilitates further work with the elemental forces. Invocation and banishing rites are also provided in case you need to invoke or banish an element for some reason. Finally, an elemental monasticism is provided. The monasticism serves to enhance your relationship with an element in a manner consistent with its nature.

Earth is heavy, dense, quiet, thick, dark, and silent. It is also very no-nonsense and practical. These characteristics have been incorporated into the rites, which are intentionally simple, to the point, and not too fancy. Many incorporate a gnosis through silence or motionlessness to be consistent with the elemental theme. Some also use the invoking and banishing elemental pentagrams (Figure 2.2). It is best to commit them to memory.

Draw towards an element's pentagram point to invoke it, and draw away from it to banish it. When drawing a pentagram in front of you it is easiest to use your head, shoulders, and hips as reference points. The topmost point will be located in front of your head, the middle points in front of your shoulders, and the bottom points in front of your hips. To draw an invoking earth pentagram the sequence is: head, left hip, right shoulder, left shoulder, right hip, and then back to your head. To draw a banishing earth pentagram, the sequence is: left hip, head, right hip, left shoulder, right shoulder, and then back to your left hip.

Figure 2.2. Elemental earth invoking and banishing pentagrams. Draw the pentagrams with your magical tool or finger. Begin at the dot and continue drawing in the direction of the arrow. When you arrive back at the dot your pentagram is complete.

invoking earth pentagram   banishing earth pentagram

Attuning with Elemental Earth

Face north in the dark at midnight, in an earthy place such as a cave, forest, or mine. A new moon in the dead of winter would be ideal. Do not wear shoes; feel the ground beneath you. If this is not practical, stand in a garden or large tray of potting soil. Practice motionlessness and silence for no less than 15 minutes. Feel the force of gravity. Feel the ground beneath you. Focus on your sense of touch and note any physical sensations you experience. Resonate with the ground beneath you and any plants or rocks in the vicinity. Physically feel the pulse of the earth rhythmically beating to the vibration of *'Adonay... 'Adonay... 'Adonay...* As time passes the vibrations grow stronger. Slowly adjust the rhythm of your body to match these vibrations. Take your time, and physically feel the vibrations. Physically feel them balancing, grounding, and stabilizing you.

Earth Entrance Rite

Statement of Intent:
It is my will to access elemental earth.

Procedure:
Face north in the dark at midnight, in an earthy place such as a cave, forest, or mine. Attune with elemental earth. Take your time and do not rush.

Draw an invoking earth pentagram on the ground (or potting soil) in front of you. Close your eyes and firmly knock on it as if you are knocking on a door. Place your open palms on your pentagram, close your eyes, and whisper:

Element of earth, in the name of *'Adonay* I greet you! Grant me access, and bestow upon me the patience, stability, and caution to use you sensibly!

Element of earth, in the name of *'Uri 'el* I greet you! Grant me access and bestow upon me the efficiency and intentionality so I may use you to prosper and be generous!

Element of earth, in the names of the *Kerubim* and *Forlak* I greet you! Protect and ground my magical and mundane lives, so I may achieve my long-term goals.

Take note of any physical sensations you feel, especially those conveyed through your sense of touch. Open your eyes and draw a triangle around your pentagram. Place your open palms on the ground slightly outside the triangle and whisper:

Gob, King of Gnomes, in the name of *'Adonay* **I evoke you! Grant me access to elemental earth and aid my efforts to obtain an earth element magical tool!**

If you do not sense Gob's presence, repeatedly whisper the evocation until you do. After you are finished communicating with him, thank him and send him on his way.

Banishing:
Banish with laughter.

Earth Element Invocation

Materials:
You will need five stones representing earth of earth, air of earth, water of earth, fire of earth, and aether of earth. Place them in the formation shown in Figure 2.3. You will be walking in a circle and picking them up during the rite. If you don't have stones draw the pentagrams with your earth tool or finger.

Figure 2.3. Earth element invocation. Place your elemental stones in the following locations beforehand – 1, earth of earth; 2, air of earth; 3, fire of earth; 4, water of earth; and 5, aether of earth. You will pick them up during the rite, starting with 1 and ending with 5. The arrows show your path of movement during the rite, as described in the text. Invocation is typically performed in a clockwise (deosil) direction.

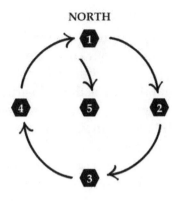

NORTH

Procedure:

1. Face north behind your earth of earth stone. Take a deep breath and center yourself. Pick up the stone and draw an invoking earth pentagram with it while whispering, *"Earth of earth, I invoke you!"* Hold onto the stone. Feel yourself becoming heavier.

2. Walk east, drawing a quarter circle from your pentagram (about chest height) until you arrive behind your air of earth stone. Face east and pick it up. Draw an invoking earth pentagram with it while whispering, *"Air of earth, I invoke you!"* Hold onto your stone. Feel yourself becoming heavier.

3. Walk south, drawing a quarter circle from your pentagram until you arrive behind your fire of earth stone. Face south and pick it up. Draw an invoking earth pentagram with it while whispering, *"Fire of earth, I invoke you!"* Hold onto your stone. Feel yourself becoming heavier.

4. Walk west, drawing a quarter circle from your pentagram until you arrive behind your water of earth stone. Face west and pick it up. Draw an invoking earth pentagram with it while whispering, *"Water of earth, I invoke you!"* Hold onto your stone. Feel yourself becoming heavier.

5. Walk north, drawing a quarter circle from your pentagram until you reach the first pentagram you drew in the north. Your circle is now complete.

6. Walk into the center of your circle. Face north behind your aether of earth stone. Draw invoking earth pentagrams above and below you while whispering, *"Aether of earth, I invoke you!"* Feel yourself becoming even heavier.

7. Close your eyes and hold the five stones to your chest for a few moments. Feel their heaviness under the force of gravity. Feel yourself becoming heavier and heavier.

8. End with a moment of silence.

Earth Element Banishing

Materials:
You will need five stones representing earth of earth, air of earth, water of earth, fire of earth, and aether of earth. You will be placing them in the formation shown in Figure 2.4 during the rite. If you don't have stones draw the pentagrams with your earth tool or finger.

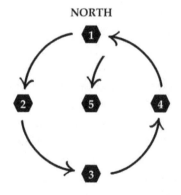

Figure 2.4. Earth element banishing. Place your elemental stones in the following locations during the rite – 1, earth of earth; 2, water of earth; 3, fire of earth; 4, air of earth; and 5, aether of earth. You will set them down during the rite, starting with 1 and ending with 5. The arrows show your path of movement during the rite, as described in the text. Banishing is typically performed in a counterclockwise (widdershins) direction.

NORTH

30

Procedure:
1. Face north while holding your five stones. Take a deep breath and center yourself. Feel how heavy the stones are. Draw a banishing earth pentagram with your earth of earth stone while saying, *"Earth of earth, I banish you!"* Set the stone on the ground in front of you. Feel yourself becoming lighter.
2. Walk west, drawing a quarter circle from your pentagram (about chest height) until you arrive in the west. Face west and draw a banishing earth pentagram with your water of earth stone while saying, *"Water of earth, I banish you!"* Set the stone on the ground in front of you. Feel yourself becoming lighter.
3. Walk south, drawing a quarter circle from your pentagram until you arrive in the south. Face south and draw a banishing earth pentagram with your fire of earth stone while saying, *"Fire of earth, I banish you!"* Set the stone on the ground in front of you. Feel yourself becoming lighter.
4. Walk east, drawing a quarter circle from your pentagram until you arrive in the east. Face east and draw a banishing earth pentagram with your air of earth stone while saying, *"Air of earth, I banish you!"* Set the stone on the ground in front of you. Feel yourself becoming lighter.
5. Walk north, drawing a quarter circle from your pentagram until you reach the first pentagram you drew in the north. Your circle is now complete.
6. Move into the center of your circle and face north. Draw banishing earth pentagrams above and below you with your aether of earth stone while saying, *"Aether of earth, I banish you!"* Set the stone on the ground. Feel yourself becoming even lighter.

7. Open your eyes widely and stretch for a few moments. Feel your lightness and mobility. Feel yourself becoming more lighthearted and cheerful.
8. End by giggling for a few seconds.

Earth Element Monasticism:

This monasticism serves to solidify and strengthen your relationship with elemental earth. The monasticism should be performed for 10 days or 10 weeks, since this number is associated with *Malkut* and material existence (Crowley, 1909/1999). However, feel free to use another earth-related number if it suits your fancy. Carry your earth tool at all times during the monasticism – this serves as a constant reminder of elemental earth and increases vigilance. After your monasticism is complete, keep your earth tool someplace special, such as an altar or favorite shelf. You may use your tool for future earth workings and reuse it if you perform the monasticism again. The Lesser Observances are accomplishable for someone who regularly has a busy schedule. The Extreme Observances are intended for someone who has extended free time. The Greater Observances are a mean between the two. The overall monasticism format is inspired by Peter J. Carroll (1992, pp. 187-90).

Beginning the Monasticism:
Face north in the dark at midnight, in an earthy place such as a cave, forest, or mine. Attune with elemental earth. Take your time and do not rush.

Draw an invoking earth pentagram on the ground in front of you. Close your eyes and firmly knock on it as if you are knocking on a door. Place your open palms on your pentagram, close your eyes, and whisper:

Element of earth, I greet you! It is my will to perform the [Lesser/Greater/Extreme] Observances of Earth for 10

[days/weeks]. This entails [whisper the appropriate sections here]. May this monasticism solidify and strengthen my relationship with you!

Lesser Observances:
1. Carry your earth tool at all times. If you can't carry it openly keep it in your pocket or a bag and carry that with you.
2. Observe a moment of silence upon waking and before going to sleep each day.
3. Perform a simple earth element rite that incorporates your tool each day.
4. Make a conscious effort to "go green" and perform at least one "green" action a day that is not already part of your normal repertoire. Visit *Zlated* (http://www.50waystohelp.com/) for suggestions.
5. Dedicate any sensory deprivation and sexual gnosis to elemental earth.

Greater Observances:
1. Perform all of the Lesser Observances.
2. Perform a second daily earth element rite that incorporates your tool.
3. Relate all of your daily meditation and magical work to elemental earth. For example, meditate on earth symbols or practice motionlessness and silence.
4. A large proportion of greenhouse gas emissions come from livestock. To combat this, abstain from eating meat. If you cannot be completely meat-free due to health reasons, reduce your intake as much as possible.

Extreme Observances:
1. Perform all of the Greater Observances.
2. Perform a third daily earth element rite that incorporates your tool.

3. Increase your efforts to "go green" as much as possible. Actions to reduce your carbon footprint can be large or small, but must be at the forefront of your consciousness. Examples include starting a compost pile, saying no to illegal wildlife products, or planting trees. Volunteer opportunities are available at *Arbor Day Foundation* (https://www. Arborday.org/), *Volunteer Match* (http://www. volunteermatch.org/), and *Conservation International* (www. conservation.org). If you want to combine your "green" efforts with tourism, there is always *GoEco* (http://www.goeco.org/).

Concluding the Monasticism:
Return to the place you began your monasticism and attune with elemental earth. Take your time and do not rush.

Draw a banishing earth pentagram on the ground in front of you. Close your eyes and firmly knock on it as if you are knocking on a door. Place your open palms on your pentagram, close your eyes, and whisper:

Element of earth, I greet you! I have performed the [Lesser/Greater/Extreme] Observances of Earth for 10 [days/weeks]. This entailed [whisper the appropriate sections here]. Though I conclude my monasticism, our relationship will endure!

Chapter 2 Homework

After taking notes on the chapter magical practice should be commenced for a minimum of 30 minutes each day for the remainder of the month. Perform the assignments in the order presented. Take your time and do not rush, especially on the earth element. It is your foundation. Remember to document your efforts in your magical diary.

1. Meditate on the topic of elemental earth for a minimum of 10 minutes each day. How does it affect your life? How do you interact with it?
2. Identify the melancholic virtues and vices you have. Classify each as having extreme, moderate, or little influence in your daily life. If you are unsure if a trait is melancholic, classify it as uncategorized. We will revisit uncategorized traits in Chapter 7. Further information about the temperaments and traits can be found at http://temperaments.fighunter.com/ and http://psychologia.co/four-temperaments/.
3. Explore different methods of gnosis. Achieve a gnostic state through at least two inhibitory and two excitatory methods.
4. Attune with elemental earth at least once daily for a period of one week.
5. Investigate the effects of the two elemental earth pentagrams. Feel free to draw a banishing pentagram after the invoking pentagram to cancel it out.
6. Perform the entrance rite. After obtaining your earth tool, purify and consecrate it by burying it in a garden or pot of salt for a few days.
7. Perform the earth element invocation and banishing rites at least once during the month. Feel free to modify them to your liking or substitute your own.
8. Establish a solid life foundation by laying the groundwork for a long-term financial plan. If you do not have a licensed financial counselor or are unsure where to begin, *Suze Orman* (http://www.suzeorman .com/), *Dave Ramsey Homepage* (http://www. daveramsey.com /home/), and *Rich Dad* (http://www. richdad. com/) are a few starting places.
9. Perform an earth element monasticism before concluding work with this element.

Chapter 3
Air Carries

Air provides the intellectual and communicative basis necessary to work with the elements. Since earth has provided our foundation our next stop is air. The alchemical and *tattva* symbols for the air element are shown in Figure 3.1. They are useful focal points in meditation and magical practice.

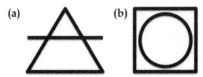

Figure 3.1. Common air element symbols. The (a) alchemical and (b) westernized *tattva* for elemental air are shown. The *tattvas* are Hindu in origin, but are occasionally used in western traditions. To make a colored image for your notes, color the *tattva* (inner circle) blue and its background (larger square) orange.

The Western View of Air

In the Greek model air is hot and wet (Aristotle, *Gen. et Corr.* 2.3, 330a30-b7, trans. 2001). Hippocratic authors write that air manifests in blood, the attractive humor (cited in Jouanna & van der Eijk, 2012). The humoral "blood" of ancient Greek medicine is different than the venous blood we recognize today (Hill, 2013). Blood predominates in spring and in those of young age (infants and children) (Page et al. (Eds.), trans. 1931/1959a; trans. 1931/1959b). The Roman physician Galen attributed a preponderance of this fluid to the sanguine temperament (cited in Arikha, 2007).

The Hermetic model expands upon the Greek model, though some differences exist. In the Hermetic view air is not considered a "true" element – it is a mediator between fire (electric) and water (magnetic) principles (Bardon, trans. 1956/2001). Air emerged naturally in response to their interactions, taking its warmth from fire and wetness from water. It is the life-giving element, as heat and moisture are necessary prerequisites for biological life. Elemental air reigns over our memory and power to judge and differentiate (Bardon, trans. 1956/2001).

The Sanguine Temperament

The preponderance of blood in the sanguine predisposes them towards optimism, confidence, and mental balance (Arikha, 2007). However, they may also be susceptible to disorganized thinking and gossip (Bardon, trans. 1956/2001). See Table 3.1 for a partial list of traits traditionally associated with the sanguine temperament.

Table 3.1. *The Sanguine Temperament*

Eysenck Traits[a]	Hermetic Virtues[b]	Hermetic Vices[b]
Sociable	Cheerful	Thoughtless
Outgoing	Independent	Boastful
Talkative	Trustful	Cunning
Responsive	Kindhearted	Conceited
Easygoing	Clever	Wasteful
Lively	Attentive	Prone to gossip
Carefree	Diligent	Easily tires
Leadership	Lucid	Dishonest

[a]Eysenck traits are adapted from *Dimensions of Personality* (Eysenck, 1947/1998). [b]Hermetic traits are adapted from *Initiation into Hermetics* (Bardon, trans. 1956/2001).

Western Air Magic

In many western esoteric traditions air is associated with communication, travel, study, visualization, finding lost objects, new beginnings, the intellect, and mental magic. In witchcraft its cardinal direction is east, its time is dawn, and its season is spring (Starhawk, 1979/1999). Our sense of smell and pastel colors are also associated with elemental air (Starhawk, 1979/1999). In witchcraft the air element is represented by the athame, sword, or censer (Starhawk, 1979/1999).

The virtue associated with elemental air is "to know" (Crowley, 1909/1999). Deities traditionally associated with elemental air include Nu (Egyptian), Zeus (Greek), Jupiter (Roman), and Vayu (Hindu).

In ceremonial traditions the air element [Heb. רוח; *ruaḥ*] is associated with the *Qabalistic* path connecting *Keter* [Crown] and *Ḥakma* [Wisdom] (Crowley, 1909/1999). It is also associated with *Yeṣirah*, the "Formative World" (Crowley, 1909/1999). This is the world of ideas and plans ready to take form (DuQuette, 2001). It is also the realm of symbols (DuQuette, 2001). It is the ו of the Tetragrammaton, the stabilization of form. Air is masculine, projective, active, gaseous, fast moving, and mental. Its *Qabalistic* King scale color is yellow, and it is the citrine of *Malkut's* citrine, olive, russet, and black (Crowley, 1909/1999;). Its traditional ceremonial tool is the dagger (Crowley, 1909/1999). The "top-down" Hebrew hierarchy, sans demons, for elemental air is shown in Table 3.2.

Table 3.2. *The Air Element Ceremonial Hierarchy*

Qabalistic World	Level	Name
אצילות [*'Aṣilut*]	Divine name	יהוה [*YHWH*][a]
בריאה [*Beri'a*]	Archangel	רפאל [*Rafa'el*]
יצירה [*Yeṣirah*]	Angelic choirs[b]	אראלים [*'Er'elim*][c]
	Angel[d]	חסן [*Ḥasan*]
	Elemental king[e]	Paralda
	Elementals[f]	Sylphs
עשיה [*'Asiya*]	Magical tool	Dagger[g]

Information is adapted from *777 Revised* (Crowley, 1909/1999). Romanized Hebrew names are in brackets. See Appendix B for pronunciations, etymologies, and more. ᵃ*Shaday ʾEl Ḥay* is "Almighty God of Life" in *Yesod.* ᵇSingular choirs are called the "elemental ruler" in many occult texts. ᶜListed as אריאל [*ʾAriʾel*] in *777 Revised* – see Appendix B for details. ᵈThe elemental angel names are written on the Seventh Pentacle of the Sun in *The Key of Solomon the King* (Mathers (Ed.), trans. 1889/2009). ᵉLévi never states the source language of the elemental king names in *Transcendental Magic: Its Doctrine and Ritual* (trans. 1896/2001). ᶠParacelsus describes the elementals in *Liber de Nymphis* (trans. 1941/1996). ᵍThe fan in some traditions.

Vibrating Divine Names

Vibratory formulas are a key magical component of many ceremonial traditions. Ancient Hermetic magicians studied sound intimately, and determined that the correct person pronouncing the correct sound in the correct tone at the correct time could bring forth profound changes in the surrounding atmosphere and universe as a whole (Flowers, 1995). Vibrating a word entails intoning it insistently and with authority so the magician resonates with its physical and spiritual "vibration" and thus its essence. Use the following steps to vibrate a divine name:

1. Visualize the word in front of you. You may embellish it with a glowing effect or flames if you'd like.
2. Inhale the word as if you are taking in a deep breath of air.
3. Intone the word upon your exhale. Use a volume and pitch that causes your entire body to physically resonate with the word. Visualize your breath reaching to the ends of the universe.

Feel free to revise the above protocol to your liking or substitute your own. When done correctly you will feel a rippling or tingling sensation throughout your body and be tired when finished. It is typically easier to begin practicing the vibratory formula with words composed of one syllable before moving on to multisyllabic words and phrases. Regarding the latter, take care to intone each syllable until you feel a physical effect before moving on to the next one.

The optimum vibratory volume and pitch varies widely among individuals. If you are female your pitch will typically be higher and your volume louder than that of your male comrades. If you have a cold it is still possible to use the vibratory formula, but you may have to change your volume and pitch to produce the desired physical effect. It also helps to embellish your inhale and exhale with additional visualizations.

Air in Chaos Magic

The air element may be applied to magical practice in numerous ways. Various egregores, godforms, or pop culture characters associated with elemental air may be invoked or evoked. Divination may be practiced via astrology, cloud watching, or observing objects moving in the wind. Paper airplanes or balloons may carry petitions into the sky. Dandelion seeds may be blown into the wind with a specific intent. Passing magical tools or other objects through incense serves to purify them. Enchanted objects may be suspended in high places. People may fan themselves to promote positive thinking or blow away negativity during magical rites.

Air is light, diffuse, sociable, thin, bright, and chatty. It is also very cheerful and optimistic. These characteristics have been incorporated into the rites, which are intentionally lively, cheerful, and dynamic. Many incorporate a gnosis through visualization, chanting, or "mental overload" to be consistent with the elemental theme. Ouranian Barbaric, a magical jargon used by chaos magicians, is also used. Magical jargons and languages serve to bypass the conscious mind so magic may work more effectively. Some of the rites also use the invoking and banishing elemental pentagrams (Figure 3.2). It is best to commit them to memory.

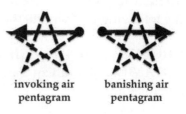

Figure 3.2. Elemental air invoking and banishing pentagrams. Draw the pentagrams with your magical tool or finger. Begin at the dot and continue drawing in the direction of the arrow. When you arrive back at the dot, your pentagram is complete.

invoking air pentagram

banishing air pentagram

Attuning with Elemental Air

Face east at dawn in a high place such as a roof or mountaintop. A windy day in the middle of spring would be ideal. Observe the surroundings from your bird's eye view. Smell the wind and its lack of density. Visualize the atmospheric particles moving rapidly and dynamically. They dart about in a playful, cheerful manner. Inhale them. Adjust the rhythm of your body to match their vibrations. The more you resonate, the lighter and more mobile you will feel. Sense these vibrations making you more spontaneous, optimistic, and fun loving.

Air Entrance Rite

Statement of Intent:
FACH DIBONGOF CHO COYANIOC CHO DIJOW ANGJABAGASS. [Ouranian Barbaric: I will to join together to the air magical current.]

Procedure:
Face east at dawn in a high place such as a roof or mountaintop. Attune with elemental air.

Draw an invoking air pentagram in the eastern sky. Visualize it strongly in your mind's eye. Vibrate *YHWH* six times. Smile and wave at the sky as if you are greeting a friend. Face your open palms towards the pentagram. Say the following and vibrate the Hebrew names:

DHOLKEY, DIJOW! FACH DIBONGOF INXMAH CHO COYANIOC. [Ouranian Barbaric: Cheers, air! I will us to join together.]

Rafa'el, GOKCHOSOD UHNGOL! JENIV UHNGOL CHO FEFPIAN, COZIJOOF, JAWENGGOJ. HUSA UHNGOL YINCAW, BUXL, EGELJACH CHO CHOYOFAQUE! [*Rafa'el*, bless me! Cure me of illness, sorrow, pain. Give me wisdom, health, clarity to do the Great Work!]

ZIXAXOXOG 'Er'elim! Ḥasan! XIQUAL AHIKAYOWFA! XIQUAL ADJCIE! XIQUAL ZAROWXICH! XIQUAL DIJOW! [Heavenly host 'Er'elim! Ḥasan! Manifest higher awareness! Manifest lightness! Manifest freedom! Manifest air!]

Take note of any physical sensations you feel, especially those conveyed through your sense of smell. Draw a triangle in the air to enclose your pentagram. Visualize it strongly and say:

Paralda, *FACH HAVAWANG HEV! XIQUAL UHNGOL BIMODANG DIJOW FIRUHL CHO CHOYOFAQUE!* [Paralda, I evoke you! Manifest me a ritual air tool to do the Great Work!]

If you do not sense Paralda's presence repeatedly chant his name until you do. After you are finished communicating with him thank him and send him on his way.

Banishing:
Banish with laughter.

Air Element Invocation

Materials:
Draw the pentagrams with your air tool or finger. If your tool is a fan open it and keep it open for the remainder of the rite.

Procedure:
1. Face east. Take a deep breath and center yourself. Draw an invoking air pentagram while saying, *"FACH LOHIXOZ DIJOW CHO DIJOW!"* [Ouranian Barbaric: I invoke air of air!] Fan the air towards you. Feel yourself becoming lighter.
2. Walk south, drawing a quarter circle from your pentagram (about chest height) until you arrive in the south. Face south and draw an invoking air pentagram while saying, *"FACH LOHIXOZ ASHARA CHO DIJOW!"* [I invoke fire of air!] Fan the air towards you. Feel yourself becoming lighter.
3. Walk west, drawing a quarter circle from your pentagram until you arrive in the west. Face west and draw an invoking air pentagram while saying, *"FACH LOHIXOZ THALDOMA CHO DIJOW!"* [I invoke water of air!] Fan the air towards you. Feel yourself becoming lighter.
4. Walk north, drawing a quarter circle from your pentagram until you arrive in the north. Face north and draw an invoking air pentagram while saying, *"FACH LOHIXOZ NOBO CHO DIJOW!"* [I invoke earth of air!] Fan the air towards you. Feel yourself becoming lighter.
5. Walk east, drawing a quarter circle from your pentagram until you reach the first pentagram you drew in the east. Your circle is now complete.
6. Walk into the center of your circle and face east. Draw invoking air pentagrams above and below you

while saying, *"FACH LOHIXOZ MEWZHIQUAL CHO DIJOW!"* [I invoke aether of air!] Fan the air towards you. Feel yourself becoming even lighter.

7. Visualize the elemental air particles around you. Inhale them. The more you inhale, the more mobile and cheerful you feel.
8. End with a high-pitched giggle.

Air Element Banishing

Materials:
Draw the pentagrams with your air tool or finger. If your tool is a fan only open it to fan away elemental air particles.

Procedure:
1. Face east. Take a deep breath and center yourself. Draw a banishing air pentagram while saying, *"FACH SCHNAFFTASI DIJOW CHO DIJOW!"* [Ouranian Barbaric: I banish air of air!] Fan the air away from you. Feel yourself becoming heavier.
2. Walk north, drawing a quarter circle from your pentagram (about chest height) until you arrive in the north. Face north and draw a banishing air pentagram while saying, *"FACH SCHNAFFTASI NOBO CHO DIJOW!"* [I banish earth of air!] Fan the air away from you. Feel yourself becoming heavier.
3. Walk west, drawing a quarter circle from your pentagram until you arrive in the west. Face west and draw a banishing air pentagram while saying, *"FACH SCHNAFFTASI THALDOMA CHO DIJOW!"* [I banish water of air!] Fan the air away from you. Feel yourself becoming heavier.
4. Walk south, drawing a quarter circle from your pentagram until you arrive in the south. Face south and draw a banishing air pentagram while saying, *"FACH SCHNAFFTASI ASHARA CHO DIJOW!"* [I

banish fire of air!] Fan the air away from you. Feel yourself becoming heavier.

5. Walk east, drawing a quarter circle from your pentagram until you reach the first pentagram you drew in the east. Your circle is now complete.

6. Walk into the center of your circle and face east. Draw banishing air pentagrams above and below you while saying, *"FACH SCHNAFFTASI MEWZHIQUAL CHO DIJOW!"* [I banish aether of air!] Fan the air away from you. Feel yourself becoming even heavier.

7. Continue fanning the elemental air out of your circle. The more you fan away, the more heavy and solemn you feel.

8. End with a moment of silence.

Air Element Monasticism

This monasticism serves to enhance your communication and relationship with elemental air. The monasticism should be performed for six days or six weeks, since this is the geomantic number associated with elemental air (Simpson, 2012). However feel free to use another air-related number if it suits your fancy. Carry your air tool at all times during the monasticism – this serves as a constant reminder of elemental air and increases vigilance. After your monasticism is complete keep your air tool someplace special, such as an altar or favorite shelf. You may use your tool for future air workings and reuse it if you perform the monasticism again. The Lesser Observances are accomplishable for someone who regularly has a busy schedule. The Extreme Observances are intended for someone who has extended free time. The Greater Observances are a mean between the two. The overall monasticism format is inspired by Peter J. Carroll (1992, pp. 187-90).

Beginning the Monasticism:
Face east at dawn in a high place such as a roof or mountaintop. Attune with elemental air.

Draw an invoking air pentagram in the eastern sky. Visualize it strongly in your mind's eye. Vibrate **YHWH** six times. Smile and wave at the sky as if you are greeting a friend. Place your open palms towards the pentagram. Say:

DHOLKEY, DIJOW! FACH DIBONGOF CHO ONGO [ICHECBAJ/ AXBIM/ DECHAHCOHIFCHEH] DIJOW LEVIFITH YODIXINCH HAGLECHOJ HUTAYAX QEBKEZ. HUSA UHNGOL YINCAW, BUXL, EGELJACH CHO CHOYOFAQUE! [Ouranian Barbaric: Cheers, air! I will to do lesser/greater/extreme air magic over a time divisible by six. Give me wisdom, health, clarity to do the Great Work!]

Lesser Observances:
1. Carry your air tool at all times. If you can't carry it openly keep it in your pocket or a bag and carry that with you.
2. Visualize an air symbol upon waking and before going to sleep each day.
3. Perform a simple air element rite that incorporates your tool each day.
4. Make a conscious effort to "broaden your horizons" by doing something new each day. It can be as simple as talking to new people, trying a new recipe, driving a different route, or reading a new book.
5. Dedicate any mental and verbal gnosis to elemental air.

Greater Observances:
1. Perform all of the Lesser Observances.
2. Perform a second daily air element rite that incorporates your tool. Your second rite should be spontaneous.

3. Relate all of your daily meditation and magical work to elemental air. For example, visualize air symbols or vibrate elemental air divine names.
4. Leave your comfort zone to "broaden your horizons" even further. Speak to people you would normally never interact with. Take a trip to a place you would normally never visit. Delve into literature or discussions supporting viewpoints you find repulsive and make an effort to understand them. Identify their logical fallacies as well as your own. Examples of logical fallacies can be found at *Thou Shalt Not Commit Logical Fallacies* (https://yourlogicalfallacyis.com/).

Extreme Observances:
1. Perform all of the Greater Observances.
2. Perform a third daily air element rite that incorporates your tool.
3. Increase your efforts to "broaden your horizons" as much as possible. Learn a new language. Become involved in your community theater. Learn to sing or dance. Fly a glider or airplane. If you are courageous enough, skydive or go bungee jumping. Travel somewhere completely new and different. The more it brings you "out of your shell," the better.

Concluding the Monasticism:
Return to the place you began your monasticism. If this is not possible choose another suitable locale. Attune with elemental air.

Smile and wave at the sky as if you are greeting a friend. Draw a banishing air pentagram in the eastern sky. Say:
DHOLKEY, DIJOW! SYCUZ! FACH DIBONGOF DONGET BICOW VYRUCH. JESNUHS! [Ouranian Barbaric: Cheers, air! It is done! I will return in the future. Thank you!]

Chapter 3 Homework

After taking notes on the chapter magical practice should be commenced for a minimum of 30 minutes each day for the remainder of the month. Perform the assignments in the order presented. Do not sacrifice quality to rush, even though air likes to do things spontaneously or in a hurry. Remember to document your efforts in your magical diary.

1. Meditate on the topic of elemental air for a minimum of 10 minutes each day. How does it affect your life? How do you interact with it?
2. Identify the sanguine virtues and vices you have. Classify each as having extreme, moderate, or little influence in your daily life. If you are unsure if a trait is sanguine classify it as uncategorized. We will revisit uncategorized traits in Chapter 7. Further information about the temperaments and traits can be found at http://temperaments.fighunter.com/ and http://psychologia.co/four-temperaments/.
3. Practice vibrating the air element divine names. What volume and pitch produce your best results? Does it work for all the words you vibrate?
4. Attune with elemental air at least once daily for a period of one week.
5. Investigate the effects of the two elemental air pentagrams. Feel free to draw a banishing pentagram after the invoking pentagram to cancel it out.
6. Perform the entrance rite. After obtaining your air tool purify and consecrate it by hanging it in a high place or passing it through incense.
7. Perform the air element invocation and banishing rites at least once during the month. Feel free to modify them to your liking or substitute your own.
8. Establish habits to improve your memory and reasoning skills. If you are unsure where to begin there are many free "brain games" available at

websites such as http://www.lumosity.com/ and http://stayingsharp.aarp.org/. Many community colleges also offer reasonably priced introductory philosophy and logic courses.

9. Perform an air element monasticism before concluding work with this element.

Chapter 4
Water Churns

Water provides the emotional and intuitive basis necessary to work with the elements. Since earth has provided our foundation and we have established a communicative basis with air, our next stop is water. The alchemical and *tattva* symbols for the water element are shown in Figure 4.1. They are useful focal points in meditation and magical practice.

(a) 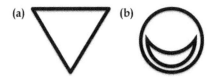 (b)

Figure 4.1. Common water element symbols. The (a) alchemical and (b) westernized *tattva* for elemental water are shown. The *tattvas* are Hindu in origin but are occasionally used in western traditions. To make a colored image for your notes color the *tattva* (inner crescent) white or silver and its background (larger circle) black.

The Western View of Water

In the Greek model water is cold and wet (Aristotle, *Gen. et Corr.* 2.3, 330a30-b7, trans. 2001). Water manifests in phlegm, the expulsive humor (cited in Jouanna & van der Eijk, 2012). Phlegm predominates in winter and in those of old age (Page et al. (Eds.), trans. 1931/1959a; trans. 1931/1959b). The Roman physician Galen attributed a preponderance of this fluid to the phlegmatic temperament (cited in Arikha, 2007).

In the Hermetic model water is one of the fundamental elements from which everything was created (Bardon, trans. 1956/2001). It is cold and contractile, the opposite of fire. The fire element emerged from the electric principle and is masculine, whereas the water element emerged from the magnetic principle and is feminine (Raleigh, 1924/1993). Harmony among the electric and magnetic principles is the "essence of good" (p. 12). Elemental water reigns over our conscience and intuition (Bardon, trans. 1956/2001).

The Phlegmatic Temperament

The preponderance of phlegm in the phlegmatic predisposes them towards acting and reacting slowly (Arikha, 2007). They may also be meek and submissive to avoid conflict (Bardon, trans. 1956/2001). See Table 4.1 for a partial list of traits traditionally associated with the phlegmatic temperament.

Table 4.1. *The Phlegmatic Temperament*

Eysenck Traits[a]	Hermetic Virtues[b]	Hermetic Vices[b]
Passive	Humble	Apathetic
Careful	Modest	Shy
Thoughtful	Compassionate	Inconsistent
Peaceful	Tender	Cold-hearted
Controlled	Forgiving	Defiant
Reliable	Abstinent	Acquiescent
Even-tempered	Content	Idle
Calm	Supportive	Shallow

[a]Eysenck traits are adapted from *Dimensions of Personality* (Eysenck, 1947/1998). [b]Hermetic traits are adapted from *Initiation into Hermetics* (Bardon, trans. 1956/2001).

Western Water Magic

In many western esoteric traditions water is associated with cleansing, healing, peacemaking, relationship, dream, psychic awareness, astral, and mirror magic. In witchcraft its cardinal direction is west, its time is sunset, and its season is autumn (Starhawk, 1979/1999). Our sense of taste and the colors blue and green are also associated with elemental water (Starhawk, 1979/1999). In witchcraft the water element is represented by the cup (Starhawk, 1979/1999).

The magical virtue associated with elemental water is "to dare" (Crowley, 1909/1999). Deities traditionally associated with elemental water include Isis (Egyptian), Poseidon (Greek), Neptune (Roman), and Apas (Hindu).

In ceremonial traditions the water element [Heb. מים; *mayim*] is associated with the *Qabalistic* path connecting *Gebura* [Strength] and *Hod* [Splendor] (Crowley, 1909/1999). It is also associated with *Beri'a*, the "Creative World" (Crowley, 1909/1999). This is the world that directly receives concepts and qualities emanated from *'Aṣilut* (DuQuette, 2001). It is the ה of the Tetragrammaton, the emergence of energy into form. Water is feminine, receptive, passive, liquid, flowing, and emotional. Its *Qabalistic* King scale color is deep blue, and it is the olive of *Malkut's* citrine, olive, russet, and black (Crowley, 1909/1999). Shades of blue-green are also associated with elemental water (Bardon, trans. 1956/2001). Its traditional ceremonial tool is the cup or chalice (Crowley, 1909/1999). The "top-down" Hebrew hierarchy, sans demons, for elemental water is shown in Table 4.2.

Table 4.2. *The Water Element Ceremonial Hierarchy*

Qabalistic World	Level	Name
אצילות [*'Aṣilut*]	Divine name	אל [*'El*][a]
בריאה [*Beri'a*]	Archangel	גבריאל [*Gavri'el*][b]
יצירה [*Yeṣirah*]	Angelic choirs[c]	תרשישים [*Tarshishim*]
	Angel[d]	טליהד [*Taliahad*]
	Elemental king[e]	Nicksa
	Elementals[f]	Undines
עשיה [*'Asiya*]	Magical tool	Cup

Information is adapted from *777 Revised* (Crowley, 1909/1999). Romanized Hebrew names are in brackets. See Appendix B for pronunciations, etymologies, and more. [a] *'Elohim Ṣeva'ot* is "God of Hosts" in *Hod*. [b] *Mika'el* in some traditions – see Appendix B for details. [c] Singular choirs are called the "elemental ruler" in many occult texts.

dThe elemental angel names are written on the Seventh Pentacle of the Sun in *The Key of Solomon the King* (Mathers (Ed.), trans. 1889/2009). eLévi never states the source language of the elemental king names in *Transcendental Magic: Its Doctrine and Ritual* (trans. 1896/2001). fParacelsus describes the elementals in *Liber de Nymphis* (trans. 1941/1996).

Cakras

Knowledge of *cakras* [San. wheels] was passed down through oral tradition and eventually documented in some of the minor Hindu *Upaniṣads* addressing yoga (e.g., *Yogakuṇḍalinī, Dhyānabindu, Śāṇḍilya...*). They serve as focal points where energy converges in the subtle body, and their use may enhance meditation and other yogic practices. The *cakras* are also relevant in some traditions of esoteric Buddhism, Daoism, and more. Thanks to the efforts of numerous scholars and translators, this knowledge became accessible to a worldwide audience.

The numbers, locales, and other attributes of *cakras* vary widely among traditions. Note that in older Hindu systems *cakras* are not attributed to particular colors, psychological functions, or spiritual states – these are completely modern. In the majority of westernized *cakra* systems, which appear to be largely based on western occultist interpretations of the *Śāradātilakatantra* and *Śivasaṃhitā*, many *cakras* are purported to exist but seven key *cakras* relating to higher consciousness are consistently recognized. These energy centers run along the spine, and the aura, an energy field surrounding the body, is sometimes considered an eighth *cakra* (Khalsa, 1998). Names and correspondences of the major *cakras* are shown in Table 4.3. If you would like to use a system more appropriate for elemental work or more consistent with your tradition for the exercises involving *cakras*, go for it.

The *cakras* have also been placed on the *Tree of Life*. The Crown corresponds to *Keter*, the Third eye to *Bina* and

Soror Velchanes

Ḥakma, the Throat to The Abyss (an imaginary line separating the top three spheres from the lower spheres), the Heart to *Gebura* and *Ḥesed*, the Solar Plexus to *Tif'eret*, the Sacral to *Neṣaḥ* and *Hod*, and the Root to *Yesod* (Kenton, n.d.). There is no *cakra* typically associated with *Malkut*.

Table 4.3 *Western Seven-cakra System Correspondences*

Cakra Name	Location	Archetype	Rules
Crown	Top of skull	Universal consciousness	Enlightenment, divine bliss
Third Eye	Forehead center (above eyebrows)	Intuition	Vision, perception
Throat	Throat	Aether	Communication, self-expression
Heart	Center of chest	Elemental air	Compassion, love, relationships
Solar Plexus	Navel	Elemental fire	Self-esteem, willpower
Sacral	Sex organs	Elemental water	Pleasure, sexuality
Root	Rectum	Elemental earth	Self-preservation instinct

Information is adapted from *Kundalini Yoga* (Khalsa, 1998). *Cakras* are listed from anterior to posterior and run along the spine.

Creating an Astral Temple

The ability to perceive and work in the astral plane enhances the effectiveness of magic. Magicians may hone their ability through skrying, lucid dreaming, constructing astral objects, crafting thought forms, and more (Ashcroft-Nowicki and Brennan, 2001; Leadbeater, 1895/2005). A plethora of literature describing the form and function of the astral plane is present in the modern day and age (see Ashcroft-Nowicki & Brennan, 2001). In a nutshell, the astral plane is the realm of dreams, imagination, thought forms, and nonmaterial existence underpinning physical reality. It is superimposed over the physical world but consists of higher vibrations (Leadbeater, 1895/2005).

Many magicians create astral temples. The astral temple serves as a private, secure place for meditation and magic. It may take weeks or months to build, and can change as you do. At minimum, your astral temple should have a pathway, an exterior, and an interior. It can be as simple or as elaborate as you want it to be – however, it is generally best to consider all five of your senses in the overall design. You may create your astral temple through meditation, ritual work, or both. Use it often. The more you use it the more powerful it will become. An example description of my old astral temple is as follows:

A sand path leads down an alley to the temple. The temple exterior is a dull, sandy color and resembles a riad. The old, heavy door has citrine, olive, russet, and black chipped paint. The door can only be opened with the astral form of my elemental water tool. Inside the atmosphere is humid and smells like a specific type of incense I've used for years. The ground is checkered with black and white tiles. The ground level is subdivided into quarters, with each one dedicated to a particular element and decorated appropriately. A set of stairs leads to rooms on upper levels. Each of them is suited for a different type of magical work, and some rooms remain unused.

Water in Chaos Magic

The water element may be applied to magical practice in numerous ways. Various egregores, godforms, or pop culture characters associated with elemental water may be invoked or evoked. Divination may be practiced via skrying in a mirror, pool, or dish of liquid. Seashells or biodegradable items may be charged and released into running water with a specific intent. Passing magical tools or other objects through naturally occurring running water serves to purify them. Images may be created in sand and then washed away by waves. People may wade or ritually bathe for cleansing or illumination purposes. They may also gaze into a magical mirror during illumination work.

Water is heavy, capricious, polymorphic, thick, dark, and mobile. It is also very emotional and intuitive. These characteristics have been incorporated into the rites, which are intentionally emotional and utilize the astral plane. Many incorporate a gnosis through emotion to be consistent with the elemental theme. Some also use the invoking and banishing elemental pentagrams (Figure 4.2). It is best to commit them to memory.

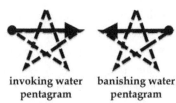

Figure 4.2. Elemental water invoking and banishing pentagrams. Draw the pentagrams with your magical tool or finger. Begin at the dot and continue drawing in the direction of the arrow. When you arrive back at the dot, your pentagram is complete.

invoking water pentagram   banishing water pentagram

Attuning with Elemental Water

Face west at sunset in a watery place such as a lake, pool, or bathtub. A full moon in the middle of autumn would be ideal. Immerse yourself as much as you are comfortable with. If the water is deep enough try to float. Feel the water moving around you and do your best to "go with the flow". Close your eyes and float around quietly for no less than 15 minutes. Feel the water moving and adapting around you. Feel how it receives your energy and impacts your emotional state. Focus on your sense of taste and note the emotional sensations you experience. Also take note of any intuitive messages you receive. Resonate with the water around you. Slowly, adjust the rhythm of your body to match these vibrations. Take your time, and emotionally feel this for as long as necessary. Sense these vibrations calming, cleansing, and accepting you.

Water Entrance Rite

Statement of Intent:
It is my will to access elemental water.

Procedure:
Face west at sunset in a watery place such as a lake, pool, or bathtub. Attune with elemental water. Take your time and do not rush.

Submerge yourself as much as you are comfortable with and draw an invoking water pentagram in the water in front of you. Come up for air as needed. Say the following in your inner (astral) voice and vibrate the Hebrew names underwater:

In the name of 'El I greet you, water, / cold, wet, and dark in the western quarter. / Raging river or vast, calm ocean, / *Gavri'el*, set the poetry of my soul in motion! / With temperance and modesty, I do dare / to practice water magic under the *Tarshishim's* care. / *Ṭaliahad*, pour into me temperance and knowing / so I may turn the tides, intuitive and flowing!

Take note of any physical sensations you feel, especially those conveyed through your sense of taste. Also take note of any intuitive messages you receive. Draw a triangle to enclose your water pentagram. Visualize it strongly and say:

I evoke you, Nicksa, undine king! / Alongside you I dare to dream, / to work with water, flow in its ways. / May it cleanse my psyche, nurture peaceful days! / Lead my

intuition towards a magical tool / to aid in my water
magic, empathetic, pure, and cool!

If you do not sense Nicksa's presence, repeatedly chant his
name until you do. After you are finished communicating
with him, thank him and send him on his way.

Banishing:
Banish with laughter.

Water Element Invocation

Face west. Take a deep breath and center yourself. Close
your eyes and imagine you are standing at the bottom of a
vast, black ocean. It is deep, dark, and completely silent.
No other living thing is present. If there were you would
feel a ripple in the water or faintly taste it.

1. Passively observe the intensity and rhythm of your
    breath. The water is cool but not uncomfortable.
    Begin to drink down the black water around you.
    The more you drink the more you become void of
    any impressions or emotions. Take a few moments to
    drink it down, filling yourself completely until you
    are a completely neutral, blank slate.
2. A silver crescent congeals from the water above you.
    It floats down and rests atop your Crown *cakra*. It is
    made of a pure silver liquid slightly heavier than the
    water around you. Draw an invoking water
    pentagram and place your hands in the shape of the
    alchemical symbol for water in front of your Sacral
    cakra.
3. Take a deep breath and vibrate *'El*. As you vibrate, the
    liquid in the *tattva* overflows, pouring down like a
    never-ending fountain. It slowly fills your Crown *cakra*.
    After your Crown *cakra* is full the liquid in it overflows,

pouring into your Third Eye *cakra*. Your Third Eye *cakra* completely fills.

4. Take another deep breath and vibrate **Gavri'el**. As you vibrate, the silver liquid overflows, pouring into your Throat *cakra*. It completely fills.
5. Take another deep breath and vibrate **Tarshishim**. As you vibrate, the silver liquid overflows, pouring into your Heart chakra. It completely fills.
6. Take another deep breath and vibrate **Ṭaliahad**. As you vibrate, the silver liquid overflows, pouring into your Solar Plexus *cakra*. After your Solar Plexus *cakra* is full the liquid in it overflows, pouring into your Sacral *cakra*. After your Sacral *cakra* is full the liquid in it overflows, pouring into your Root *cakra*. It completely fills.
7. Take a deep breath and vibrate **mayim**. As you vibrate, the silver liquid overflows, gradually filling up your entire body and aura.
8. You are a small silver drop in a vast, black ocean. Feel the emptiness and the calmness. Outstretch your hands and say, *"Before me water, behind me water, at my right hand water, at my left hand water. Above me, below me, and inside of me water!"*
9. Open your eyes.

Water Element Banishing

1. Face west. Take a deep breath and center yourself. Close your eyes and imagine you are standing at the bottom of a vast, black ocean. It is deep, dark, and completely silent. No other living thing is present. If there were you would feel a ripple in the water or faintly taste it.
2. Passively observe the intensity and rhythm of your breath. The water is cool but not uncomfortable. Begin to drink down the black water around you. The

more you drink, the more you become void of any impressions or emotions. Take a few moments to drink it down, filling yourself completely until you are a completely neutral blank slate.

3. Draw a banishing water pentagram in front of you. A tiny air bubble emerges from the center of this pentagram. It floats over, eventually resting atop your Crown *cakra*. The bubble feels warm and light. With each breath the air bubble will expand, eventually encompassing your entire body. You will feel progressively warmer and lighter as it grows.

4. The tiny air bubble slowly grows and surrounds your Crown *cakra*. As you continue to breathe the bubble expands more and surrounds your Third Eye *cakra*. The space inside the bubble is warm and hollow, filled with air.

5. The bubble expands with each breath you take. It now surrounds your Throat *cakra* and body from the neck up. The parts of you inside the bubble feel warm and hollow. You also feel a bit lighter than before.

6. The bubble expands with each breath you take. It now surrounds your Heart *cakra* and body from the chest up. The parts of you inside the bubble feel warm and hollow. You also feel a bit lighter than before.

7. The bubble expands with each breath you take. It now surrounds your Solar Plexus, Sacral, and Root *cakras*. From the hips up you feel warm and hollow. You are feeling much lighter and more cheerful now.

8. The bubble expands with each breath you take. Now it envelops your upper legs, knees, lower legs, and feet. You are feeling much lighter and more cheerful now.

9. The bubble expands, completely enveloping you. Inside it is light, hollow, and cheerful. The bubble ascends slowly, carrying you to the ocean's surface. As you float higher and higher, the bubble accelerates.

10. When you reach the surface the bubble rests for a moment. It continues expanding around you, pushing the black water further and further away. The water eventually leaves your field of vision.

11. Smell and taste the empty space around you. Outstretch your hands and say, *"Before me emptiness, behind me air, at my right hand earth, at my left hand fire. Above me, below me, and inside me are earth, air, and fire!"*

12. Open your eyes, clap, and laugh!

Water Element Monasticism

This monasticism serves to cleanse and nurture your relationship with elemental water. The monasticism should be performed for four days or four weeks, since this is the geomantic number associated with elemental water (Simpson, 2012). However, feel free to use another water-related number if it suits your fancy. Carry your water tool at all times during the monasticism – this serves as a constant reminder of elemental water and increases vigilance. After your monasticism is complete keep your water tool someplace special, such as an altar or favorite shelf. You may use your tool for future water workings and reuse it if you perform the monasticism again. The Lesser Observances are accomplishable for someone who regularly has a busy schedule. The Extreme Observances are intended for someone who has extended free time. The Greater Observances are a mean between the two. The overall monasticism format is inspired by Peter J. Carroll (1992, pp. 187-90).

Beginning the Monasticism:
Face west at sunset in a wet place such as a lake, pool, or bathtub. Attune with elemental water. Take your time and do not rush.

Submerge yourself as much as you are comfortable with and draw an invoking water pentagram in the water in front of you. Come up for air as needed. Say the following in your inner (astral) voice:

I hail you water, this tranquil evening! / With the start of my monasticism, I send this greeting. / A raging river, or a vast, calm ocean, / I dare to practice your magic, test my devotion. / May the lesser/greater/extreme observances temper, cleanse, and develop my intuition. / I will to nurture my relationship with you; this is my intention!

Lesser Observances:
1. Carry your water tool at all times. If you can't carry it openly keep it in your pocket or a bag and carry that with you.
2. Contemplate your relationship with elemental water when you take a bath or shower each day.
3. Perform a simple water element rite that incorporates your tool each day.
4. Keep a dream diary beside your bed. Upon waking, recall your dreams and write them down. Many magicians keep the dream diary separate from the magical diary, as it can get voluminous. Important entries can be referenced in or transferred into the primary diary.
5. Dedicate any emotional gnosis to elemental water.

Greater Observances:
1. Perform all of the Lesser Observances.
2. Perform a second daily water element rite that incorporates your tool. Your second rite should be performed in your astral temple.

3. Relate all of your daily meditation and magical work to elemental water. For example, contemplate water symbols or practice divination to sharpen your intuition.
4. Learn to lucid dream. Primers can be found at *The Lucidity Institute* (http://www.lucidity.com/) and *How To Lucid* (http://howtolucid.com/). If you prefer a print resource, *Lucid Dreams in 30 Days* by Keith Harry and Pamela Weintraub is an excellent book that my magical comrades and I have used with great success.

Extreme Observances:
1. Perform all of the Greater Observances.
2. Perform a third daily water element rite that incorporates your tool.
3. Learn to perform astral projection. Primers can be found at *Jeff Finley* (http://jefffinley.org/obe/) and *AstralHQ* (http://astralhq.com/astral-projection-guide/). Often times it takes a while to get good at it.

Concluding the Monasticism:
Return to the place you began your monasticism and attune with elemental water. Take your time and do not rush.

Submerge yourself as much as you are comfortable with and draw a banishing water pentagram in the water in front of you. Come up for air as needed. Say the following in your inner (astral) voice:

I hail you water, this tranquil evening! / With the conclusion of my monasticism, I send this greeting. / A raging river, or a vast, calm ocean, / I dared to practice your magic, test my devotion. / Though my monasticism now comes to an end, / our future work has yet to begin!

Chapter 4 Homework

After taking notes on the chapter magical practice should be commenced for a minimum of 30 minutes each day for the remainder of the month. Perform the assignments in the order presented. Do not become discouraged if your productivity level fluctuates, as elemental water does not always flow at a steady pace. Remember to document your efforts in your magical diary.

1. Meditate on the topic of elemental water for a minimum of 10 minutes each day. How does it affect your life? How do you interact with it?
2. Identify the phlegmatic virtues and vices you have. Classify each as having extreme, moderate, or little influence in your daily life. If you are unsure if a trait is phlegmatic, classify it as uncategorized. We will revisit uncategorized traits in Chapter 7. Further information about the temperaments and traits can be found at http://temperaments.fighunter.com/ and http://psychologia.co/four-temperaments/.
3. Create an astral temple. It should have a pathway, an exterior, and an interior. Incorporate all five of your senses in the overall design. The more frequently you use your astral temple the more powerful it will become.
4. Attune with elemental water at least once daily for a period of one week.
5. Investigate the effects of the two elemental water pentagrams. Feel free to draw a banishing pentagram after the invoking pentagram to cancel it out.
6. Perform the entrance rite. After obtaining your water tool, purify and consecrate it by washing it in naturally occurring running water.
7. Perform the water element invocation and banishing rites at least twice during the month. Feel free to modify them to your liking or substitute your own.

Perform them in your usual spot the first time. The second time, perform them in your astral temple. Compare and contrast your experiences in each setting.

8. Begin to clear out all the subconscious rubbish you have. This tends to be unpleasant. Introspection, meditation, magical work, counseling, and more can be used to jumpstart this process. Identifying the rubbish fragments can be challenging. Getting rid of them may be even more difficult.

9. Perform a water element monasticism before concluding work with this element.

Chapter 5
Fire Burns

Fire provides the passion and willpower necessary to work with the elements. Since earth has provided our foundation, air has established a communicative basis, and water has cultivated our intuition, our next stop is fire. The alchemical and *tattva* symbols for the fire element are shown in Figure 5.1. They are useful focal points in meditation and magical practice.

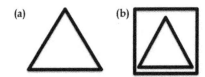

Figure 5.1. Common fire element symbols. The (a) alchemical and (b) westernized *tattva* for elemental fire are shown. The *tattvas* are Hindu in origin but are occasionally used in western traditions. To make a colored image for your notes color the *tattva* (inner triangle) red and its background (larger square) green.

The Western View of Fire

In the Greek model fire is hot and dry (Aristotle, *Gen. et Corr.* 2.3, 330a30-b7, trans. 2001). Fire manifests in yellow bile, the digestive humor (cited in Jouanna & van der Eijk, 2012). Yellow bile predominates in summer and in youth (Page et al. (Eds.), trans. 1931/1959a; trans. 1931/1959b). The Roman physician Galen attributed a preponderance of this fluid to the choleric temperament (cited in Arikha, 2007).

In the Hermetic model fire is one of the fundamental elements from which everything was created (Bardon, trans. 1956/2001). It is hot and expansive, the opposite of water. Light is an aspect of fire, whereas darkness is an aspect of water. Fire is also intimately connected with light. In many creation stories light is followed by fire (see Ede, 2006). Elemental fire reigns over our energy, might, and passion (Bardon, trans. 1956/2001).

The Choleric Temperament

The preponderance of yellow bile in the choleric predisposes them towards enthusiasm and bravery (Arikha, 2007). However, they may also be excessively aggressive and argumentative (Bardon, trans. 1956/2001). See Table 5.1 for a partial list of traits traditionally associated with the choleric temperament.

Table 5.1. *The Choleric Temperament*

Eysenck Traits[a]	Hermetic Virtues[b]	Hermetic Vices[b]
Touchy	Enthusiastic	Quick tempered
Restless	Daring	Jealous
Aggressive	Courageous	Hateful
Excitable	Determined	Vengeful
Changeable	Brave	Angry
Impulsive	Eager	Argumentative
Optimistic	Creative	Self destructive
Active	Assiduous	Immoderate

[a]Eysenck traits are adapted from *Dimensions of Personality* (Eysenck, 1947/1998). [b]Hermetic traits are adapted from *Initiation into Hermetics* (Bardon, trans. 1956/2001).

Western Fire Magic

In many western esoteric traditions fire is associated with purification, protection, banishing, destruction, empowering, war, career, and candle magic. Our ancestors were mesmerized by the power of fire and many considered it a senior element (Wolfe, 1998). In witchcraft its cardinal direction is south, its time is noon, and its season is summer (Starhawk, 1979/1999). Our sense of sight and the colors red and orange are also associated with elemental fire (Starhawk,

1979/1999). In witchcraft the fire element is represented by the wand or censer (Starhawk, 1979/1999).

The magical virtue associated with elemental fire is "to will" (Crowley, 1909/1999). Deities traditionally associated with elemental fire include Mau (Egyptian), Hades (Greek), Pluto (Roman), and Agni (Hindu).

In ceremonial traditions the fire element [Heb. אש; 'esh] is associated with the *Qabalistic* path connecting *Hod* [Splendor] and *Malkut* [Kingdom] (Crowley, 1909/1999). It is also associated with *'Aṣilut*, the "Archetypal World" (Crowley, 1909/1999). This is the world of pure principles and archetypes (DuQuette, 2001). It is the ' of the Tetragrammaton, primal energy. Fire is masculine, projective, active, plasma-like, expansive, and willful. Its *Qabalistic* King scale color is glowing orange scarlet, and it is the russet of *Malkut's* citrine, olive, russet, and black (Crowley, 1909/1999). Red in general is also associated with elemental fire (Bardon, trans. 1956/2001). Its traditional ceremonial tool is the wand (Crowley, 1909/1999). The "top-down" Hebrew hierarchy, sans demons, for elemental fire is shown in Table 5.2.

Table 5.2. *The Fire Element Ceremonial Hierarchy*

Qabalistic World	Level	Name
אצילות [*'Aṣilut*]	Divine name	אלהים [*'Elohim*]a
בריאה [*Beri'a*]	Archangel	מיכאל [*Mika'el*]b
יצירה [*Yeṣirah*]	Angelic choirsc	שרפים [*Serafim*]
	Angeld	אריאל [*'Ari'el*]
	Elemental kinge	Djîn
	Elementalsf	Salamanders
עשיה [*'Asiya*]	Magical tool	Wandg

Information is adapted from *777 Revised* (Crowley, 1909/1999). Romanized Hebrew names are in brackets. See Appendix B for pronunciations, etymologies, and more. aYHWH Ṣeva'ot is "LORD of Hosts" in Neṣaḥ. bGavri'el in some traditions – see Appendix B for details. cSingular choirs are called the "elemental ruler" in many occult texts. dThe elemental angel names are written on the Seventh Pentacle of the Sun in *The Key of Solomon the King* (Mathers (Ed.), trans.

1889/2009). eLévi never states the source language of the elemental king names in *Transcendental Magic: Its Doctrine and Ritual* (trans. 1896/2001). fParacelsus describes the elementals in *Liber de Nymphis* (trans. 1941/1996). gThe lamp in some traditions.

Will with a Capital "W"

Crowley defines magic as "the art and science of causing change to occur in conformity with Will" (quoted in Reid, 1996, p. 150). When you perform an act of Will you are carrying out an action consciously and intentionally. Your Will has the potential to transform mundane acts such as pouring tea, checking your mail, or cleaning your home into magical acts. *The Magician's Dictionary* (Rehmus, 1990) states Will is:

> ...*another word for persistence and maintained attention. Will is one of the two natural human powers for altering reality (the other is Imagination). When faced with an insoluble problem or great odds against us, it is the Will alone that leads us through to solution and victory. As the Imagination is the power of the mind through understanding and enlightenment, the Will is the way of material action. There is no will without physical effort of some kind exerted over physical phenomena.* (p. 281)

In the Thelemic paradigm a person's True Will is their grand destiny in life. It is said that when you are carrying out your True Will you will have the momentum of the universe behind you because you are working in harmony with it.

Fire in Chaos Magic

The fire element may be applied to magical practice in numerous ways. Various egregores, godforms, or pop culture characters associated with elemental fire may be invoked or evoked. Divination may be practiced via interpreting the ashes of a fire or by pyromancy. Flammable items may be charged and then burned. Passing magical tools or other objects through flames serves to purify them. Sigils or petitions may be written on paper and then ritually ignited. People may consume spicy foods during purification, exorcism, or illumination rites. They may also walk across hot coals or bask in the sun during magical rites.

Fire is light, creative, quick, thin, bright, and volatile. It is also very zealous and willful. These characteristics have been incorporated into the rites, which are intentionally short, energetic, and hard-hitting. Many incorporate a gnosis through gazing or heat to be consistent with the elemental theme. Some also use the invoking and banishing elemental pentagrams (Figure 5.2). It is best to commit them to memory.

Figure 5.2. Elemental fire invoking and banishing pentagrams. Draw the pentagrams with your magical tool or finger. Begin at the dot and continue drawing in the direction of the arrow. When you arrive back at the dot, your pentagram is complete.

invoking fire
pentagram

banishing fire
pentagram

Attuning with Elemental Fire

Face south at noon in front of a lit candle, fireplace, or bonfire. Gaze into the flames. Feel the heat and dryness they emanate. Resonate with their ambitious, expansive nature, and will yourself to match these vibrations. Feel yourself expanding and getting warmer, becoming more lively and energetic. Note any sensations you feel, particularly those conveyed through your sense of sight. Also take note of any creative ideas or inspiration you receive.

If you are using a candle, pinch or snuff out the flame when finished. Do not blow it out. In many traditions manually blowing out a candle flame is interpreted as insulting fire with air. If you are using a fireplace or bonfire, let the flames die out naturally.

Fire Entrance Rite

Materials:
You will need a lit candle, fireplace, or bonfire. You will also need a hot pepper.

Statement of Intent:
It is my will to access elemental fire.

Procedure:
Face south at noon in front of a lit candle, fireplace, or bonfire. Attune with elemental fire.

Gaze into the flames and draw an invoking fire pentagram from a safe distance. Strongly visualize it in front of the flames. Bite into your hot pepper. Leave the pepper in your mouth for as long as you can stand it during the remainder of the rite. Place your open palms towards the flames to feel their heat. Gaze into the flames. Boldly say the following and vibrate the Hebrew names, visualizing strongly upon your exhales:

Element of fire, in the name of *'Elohim* I greet you! I will to access you! In the name of *Mika'el*, ignite my inner fire so I may accomplish my True Will! In the name of the *Serafim*, burn away the vices that hinder me! In the name of *'Ari'el*, impassion me with courage, determination, and ardency!

Take note of any physical sensations you feel, especially those conveyed through your sense of sight. Also take note of any creative ideas or inspiration you receive. Draw a triangle to enclose your fire pentagram – this may be done physically or through visualization. Gaze into the flames and boldly say:

Djîn, King of Salamanders, in the name of ʾElohim I evoke you! I will to access elemental fire! Assist me in obtaining a magical tool that will inspire work with this element!

If you do not sense Djîn's presence repeatedly chant his name and dance around enthusiastically until you do. After you are finished communicating with him thank him and send him on his way.

Banishing:
Banish with laughter. If you are using a candle, pinch or snuff out the flame. If you are using a fireplace or bonfire, let the flames die out naturally.

Fire Element Invocation

Materials:
Draw the pentagrams with your finger if you do not have a fire tool. Additional items you associate with elemental fire such as hot peppers, candles, or energetic music may also be included. There is a spontaneous component to this rite.

Procedure:
Face south. Take a deep breath and center yourself. As you breathe visualize the elemental fire inside of you and in your immediate environment. Visualize it intensely, until you see it as clearly as everything else.

Draw an invoking fire pentagram and shout, *"Elemental fire, I invoke you!"* Inhale the elemental fire. See it concentrating in your body and feel yourself becoming warmer. You may also bite into a hot pepper, dance around, and perform any other actions you'd like. The more instinctive they are, the better. You have invoked sufficient elemental fire when you feel warm and energetic.

Fire Element Banishing

Materials:
Draw the pentagrams with your finger if you do not have a fire tool.

Procedure:
Face south. Take a deep breath and center yourself. As you breathe visualize the elemental fire inside of you and in your immediate environment. Visualize it intensely, until you see it as clearly as everything else.

Draw a banishing fire pentagram and shout, *"Elemental fire, I banish you!"* Visualize yourself exhaling elemental fire. See it leaving your body. Feel yourself becoming cooler and more lethargic. You may also shoo away the elemental fire in your immediate environment. You have banished sufficient elemental fire when you feel cooler and less energetic.

Fire Element Monasticism

This monasticism serves to impassion and expand your relationship with elemental fire. The monasticism should be performed for five days or five weeks, since this is the geomantic number associated with elemental fire (Simpson, 2012). However feel free to use another fire-related number if it suits your fancy. Carry your fire tool at all times during the monasticism – this serves as a constant reminder of elemental fire and increases vigilance. After your monasticism is complete keep your fire tool someplace special, such as an altar or favorite shelf. You may use your tool for future fire workings and reuse it if you perform the monasticism again. The Lesser Observances are accomplishable for someone who regularly has a busy schedule. The Extreme Observances are intended for someone who has extended free time. The Greater Observances are a mean between the two. The overall monasticism format is inspired by Peter J. Carroll (1992, pp. 187-90).

Beginning the Monasticism:
Face south at noon in front of a lit candle, fireplace, or bonfire. Attune with elemental fire.

Gaze into the flames and draw an invoking fire pentagram from a safe distance. Strongly visualize it in front of the flames. Bite into a hot pepper if you have one handy. Leave the pepper in your mouth for as long as you can stand it during the remainder of the rite. Place your open palms towards the flames to feel their heat. Gaze into the flames and boldly say:

Element of fire, I greet you! It is my will to perform the [Lesser/Greater/Extreme] Observances of Fire for five [days/weeks]. This entails [boldly say the appropriate sections here]. May this monasticism impassion and expand my relationship with you!

Lesser Observances:
1. Carry your fire tool at all times. If you can't carry it openly keep it in your pocket or a bag and carry that with you.
2. Bask in the sun for a few minutes each day while contemplating your relationship with elemental fire. Use sunscreen and do not stare directly at the sun!
3. Perform a simple fire element rite that incorporates your tool each day.

4. Meditate on the concept of True Will each day. Contemplate how you may discover and carry out yours.
5. Dedicate any gazing and physical exhaustion gnosis to elemental fire.

Greater Observances:
1. Perform all of the Lesser Observances.
2. Perform a second daily fire element rite that incorporates your tool. Your second rite should be short but intense.
3. Relate all of your daily meditation and magical work to elemental fire. For example, gaze into a candle flame or contemplate your True Will.
4. Optimize your life so you may discover and carry out your True Will. Which thoughts, emotions, and habits are helping you? Which are hindering you? Document your efforts and any insights in your magical diary.

Extreme Observances:
1. Perform all of the Greater Observances.
2. Perform a third daily fire element rite that incorporates your tool.
3. Make every act an act of Will. Consciously choose and willfully experience your thoughts, feelings, words, movements, actions, and reactions. How many of them are aligned with your True Will? Hold yourself accountable. Resist the urge to go through your day on "mental autopilot," blindly following established routines. The more you practice this, the less exhausting it will become.

Concluding the Monasticism:
Return to the place you began your monasticism and attune with elemental fire. When ready, gaze into the

flames and draw a banishing fire pentagram at a safe distance. Gaze into the flames and boldly say:

Element of fire, I greet you! I willed to perform the [Lesser/Greater/Extreme] Observances of Fire for five [days/weeks]. This entailed [boldly say the appropriate sections here]. Though I conclude my monasticism, our relationship will expand!

Chapter 5 Homework

After taking notes on the chapter magical practice should be commenced for a minimum of 30 minutes each day for the remainder of the month. Perform the assignments in the order presented. Fire is enthusiastic and ambitious. Exercise caution and avoid taking on everything at once. Remember to document your efforts in your magical diary.

1. Meditate on the topic of elemental fire for a minimum of 10 minutes each day. How does it affect your life? How do you interact with it?
2. Identify the choleric virtues and vices you have. Classify each as having extreme, moderate, or little influence in your daily life. If you are unsure if a trait is choleric classify it as uncategorized. We will revisit uncategorized traits in Chapter 7. Further information about the temperaments and traits can be found at http://temperaments.fighunter.com/ and http://psychologia.co/four-temperaments/.
3. Reflect on the concepts of Will with a capital "W" and True Will. How do they impact your life? Are you carrying out your True Will now? If not, why?
4. Attune with elemental fire at least once daily for a period of one week.

5. Investigate the effects of the two elemental fire pentagrams. Feel free to draw a banishing pentagram after the invoking pentagram to cancel it out.

6. Perform the entrance rite. After obtaining your fire tool, purify and consecrate it by passing it through flames.

7. Perform the fire element invocation and banishing rites at least once during the month. Feel free to modify them to your liking or substitute your own.

8. Reflect on long-term goals you will to accomplish in life. List them in your magical diary and develop a written plan to move forward. Document your plan, progress, insights, and any revisions in your diary.

9. Perform a fire element monasticism before concluding work with this element.

Chapter 6
The Elements Together

So far we have explored the terrestrial elements, internalized them, and determined how they impact our lives. We have also interacted with them magically. In ancient Greek and Hermetic models the elements form material existence, impact our heath, and influence our personality (Arikha, 2007; Bardon, trans. 1956/2001; Copenhaver (Trans.), 1995). Pairs of elements that share no binary properties (earth and air, water and fire) are considered opposites. Here, we will more scrupulously examine elemental interactions and how they may help us achieve harmony, health, and life balance.

The Pentagram Revisited

The invoking and banishing elemental pentagrams follow a general formula. To invoke an element, trace towards its pentagram point. To banish an element, trace away from it. The placement of the elements on the pentagram is worth meditating upon – an additional layer of relationships will be revealed. For example, invoking water and banishing air pentagrams are drawn using the same procedure, as are banishing water and invoking air pentagrams. The topmost point of the pentagram represents aether (Crowley, 1909/1999), which we will explore in the following chapter. Aether has no single commonly accepted alchemical symbol, but is frequently represented by a circle. Traditional assignments of the elements to each pentagram point are shown in Figure 6.1.

Figure 6.1. The pentagram. Elements are denoted by their alchemical symbols and placed on their corresponding pentagram points, as given in *777 Revised* (Crowley, 1909/1999).

Thinking in Fours

There are several sets of four present in nature. There are four cardinal directions, seasons, times of day, commonly encountered states of matter, and more. There are also many sets of four present in western culture. Many of these "fours" hold magical significance– each member of a set reflects the qualities of a specific element, with all four elements being ultimately represented. This is how magical correspondences are produced. Traditional western magical correspondences previously discussed for each element are shown in Table 6.1.

Table 6.1. *Traditional Western Magical Correspondences of the Four Elements*

Attribute	Earth	Air	Water	Fire
Cardinal direction[a]	North	East	West	South
Season	Winter	Spring	Autumn	Summer
Time of day	Midnight	Dawn	Dusk	Noon
State of matter	Solid	Gas	Liquid	Plasma
Magical virtue	To keep silent	To know	To dare	To will

Information is adapted from the previous chapters. Note that alternate correspondence schemes with equally valid rationales exist. [a]Cardinal directions for the northern hemisphere are shown.

Correspondences such as these are commonly used to enhance magical work. You may incorporate as many or as few of them into your practice as you'd like. The ability to "think in fours" will permit you to produce your own personally significant elemental correspondences. What other fours in nature or western culture can you think of? Which element would you assign to each member of a set and why? Example rationales justifying the correspondences in Table 6.1 are as follows:

Cardinal Directions:
Traditional correspondences for each cardinal direction reflect European geography. As you travel north away from the equator average temperatures decrease and snow and ice become more abundant. This reflects elemental earth, which is cold and dry. As you travel south towards the equator average temperatures increase and there are less drastic changes in sunlight levels throughout the year. This reflects elemental fire, which is hot and dry. Travelling east through the Central Russian Upland leads to the Ural Mountains. Mountains are associated with air in many traditions. Travelling west ultimately leads to the Atlantic Ocean, which reflects elemental water.

In some family traditions I have seen magicians assign different elements to each cardinal direction. In these scenarios, it is typically done to reflect local geography. For example, if you live in the Southern Hemisphere you may assign fire to the north and earth to the south, as the equator is located to your north instead of your south. If you have a mountain range to your west and a large body of water to your east, you may assign air to the west and water to the east. Whatever you choose, it should make sense to you and be internally consistent with whatever system you are using.

Seasons:
Traditional correspondences for each season reflect trends in relative temperatures and sunlight levels. The closer to the equator you live, the less dramatic these changes are. Winter is characterized by the coldest average

temperatures and least amount of daytime sunlight. Liquid water becomes less abundant in regions that experience freezing weather. This reflects elemental earth, which is cold and dry. During spring, average temperatures and daily sunlight levels increase. New plants may grow as the ground thaws. This reflects elemental air, which is hot and wet. This is also why elemental air and the spring season are associated with new beginnings. Summer is characterized by the hottest average temperatures and greatest amount of daytime sunlight. This reflects elemental fire, which is hot and dry. During autumn, average temperatures and daily sunlight levels decrease. This reflects elemental water, which is cold and wet.

Times of Day:
Traditional correspondences for each time of day reflect trends in relative daily temperatures and sunlight levels. Midnight features the coldest average temperatures and complete lack of sunlight. This reflects elemental earth, which is cold and dry. At dawn, average temperatures and sunlight levels begin to increase. This reflects elemental air, which is hot and wet. At noon, average temperatures and sunlight levels are highest. This reflects elemental fire, which is hot and dry. At dusk, average temperatures and sunlight levels begin to decrease. This reflects elemental water, which is cold and wet.

States of Matter:
The four most commonly encountered states of matter are solids, liquids, gases, and plasma. Solids are the densest of the group, and earth is the densest of the elements. If you are a physics enthusiast, Bose-Einstein condensate also reflects some qualities of elemental earth. Elemental water is associated with the liquid state of matter, as we most commonly see water in its liquid form. Following the same line of thinking, elemental air corresponds to the gaseous

state of matter. Gas particles move stochastically and dynamically, as does elemental air. Plasma is the hottest and most energetic of the group, as is elemental fire. The hot, ionized particles that characterize this state of matter are most commonly seen in lightning.

Magical Virtues:
Lévi's Four Powers of the Sphinx are to know, to will, to dare, and to keep silent (trans. 1896/2001). These virtues are typically assigned as corresponding to air, fire, water, and earth, respectively (Crowley, 1909/1999). However, note that alternate correspondence schemes with equally valid rationales exist (see Crowley, 1944/2004; Wolfe, 1998). Lévi writes, "In order to command the elements, we must have overcome their hurricanes, their lightnings, their abysses, their tempests. In order TO DARE we must KNOW; in order to WILL, we must DARE; we must WILL to possess empire and to reign we must BE SILENT" (trans. 1896/2001, p. 202).

Elemental air rules over the mental aspect of our daily lives. It provides lucidity and sharpens our critical thinking skills at its best, enabling our quest for accurate, objective knowledge. Elemental fire rules over the career aspect of our daily lives. It drives us to create and innovate at its best. It also impassions us with the motivation and enthusiasm necessary to exert our will upon the universe. Elemental water rules over the emotional aspect of our daily lives. It fosters our compassion and intuition at its best. Elemental earth rules over the monetary and material aspect of our daily lives. It is also the quietest and steadiest of the bunch.

Elemental Balance

Removing a member from its set of four would result in disparity and imbalance, as the universe would not be able to fully express itself. Likewise, the elements coexist and work together in a balanced manner. The overarching theme of maintaining balance among the elements recurs in numerous western cosmological models and esoteric traditions (Arikha, 2007; Bardon, trans. 1956/2001; Conway, 2005; Carrick, 2001).

The Elements and Health

In the humoral model developed by Hippocratic authors (Page et al. (Eds.), trans. 1931/1959a; trans. 1931/1959b) and expanded by Galen (see Arikha, 2007), the humors (body fluids) are the bearers of elemental properties in the human body. The quantities of black bile, blood, phlegm, and yellow bile within us are responsible for our good health or lack thereof (Page et al. (Eds.), trans. 1931/1959a; trans. 1931/1959b). The optimum quantity of each humor varies between individuals, and also fluctuates according to season, age, and lifestyle (trans. 1931/1959a; trans. 1931/1959b). Disease originates from three major sources: excess or deficiency of the elements through improper diet, forceful causes (such as falls, wounds, or fatigue), and environmental conditions (Carrick, 2001).

Treatment under the humoral model focuses on restoring elemental balance (Carrick, 2001; Jouanna & van der Eijk, 2012). Physicians prescribed various diet and exercise regimens to alleviate symptoms and bring the humors back into equilibrium (Page et al. (Eds.), trans. 1931/1959c). Emetics or laxatives were also prescribed if deemed necessary (trans. 1931/1959b; trans. 1931/1959d). Another possibility was Galen's famous *theriac*, an herbal remedy alleged to cure all ailments and diseases (Tibi, 2006). Opium was likely its only active ingredient. More extreme treatments such as bloodletting were also not out of the question. Bloodletting was practiced widely in the ancient world and through the 1800s in an effort to rid the body of impurities (Carrick, 2001; Hill, 2013). Many famous people died from bloodletting or its complications, including King Charles II of England and United States President George Washington (Hill, 2013).

The Elements and Psychology

Health and personality are not decoupled in the humoral model (Arikha, 2007; Carrick, 2001; Jouanna & van der Eijk, 2012; Page et al. (Eds.), trans. 1931/1959e). The humors influence the overall temperament, as you explored in previous chapters. Each individual is composed of a unique elemental constitution (Bardon, trans. 1956/2001; Page et al. (Eds.), trans. 1931/1959a; trans. 1931/1959b). A preponderance of traits attributed to one or two temperaments may dominate the personality, or traits may be fairly evenly dispersed across all temperament types. You may exhibit more virtues or vices associated with some temperaments, whereas others have a more even distribution. Everyone is different, and there is no "best" temperament. Document new traits in your magical diary when you discover them, so you have the most up-to-date records possible. Questions for reflection before undertaking any further elemental work are as follows:

1. Sum up your total traits (virtues + vices) for each temperament category. Do one or two temperament types dominate your personality, or are the traits fairly evenly distributed across temperaments?
2. Within each temperament type, do you exhibit more virtues or more vices? Are there any temperaments where virtues and vices are fairly evenly distributed?
3. Do any traits suggest overbalance or underbalance of an element?

Elemental overbalance (too much of an element) and underbalance (not enough of an element) are not uncommon. Traits associated with one element may be highly developed to compensate for underdeveloped ones (Greene, 1978). This is much like when diminishment or loss of one sense results in enhancement of other senses to compensate. Evidence of too much or not enough of a particular element manifest in a manner consistent with that element's nature. A non-exhaustive list of traits associated with elemental overbalance or underbalance is outlined below. Information is adapted from Wynn-Jones (2015):

Earth:

Those with an excess of elemental earth may be boring, materialistic, or have tunnel vision. Those lacking enough elemental earth may be careless, unreliable, or tasteless.

Air:

Those with an excess of elemental air may be chatterboxes, shallow, or overanalyze everything. Those lacking enough elemental air may be slow, have muddy thinking, or communicate ineffectively.

Water:

Those with an excess of elemental water may be depressed or hypersensitive. Those lacking enough elemental water may be emotionally cold.

Fire:

Those with an excess of elemental fire may be egotistical, violent, or dominating. Those lacking enough elemental fire may be unenergetic, bored, or have an inferiority complex.

Though the four humors doctrine is obsolete in modern evidence-based medicine and psychology, it did lay the groundwork for subsequent personality theories. Categorizing the hallmark traits of each temperament as introvert/extrovert and emotionally stable/unstable, as given in Hans Eysenck's

Dimensions of Personality (1947), results in groupings reflective of Galen-Kant-Wundt descriptions of people (Miles & Hempel, 2004). In their analysis, more active, sociable, and assertive individuals are classified as more extroverted. In addition, more unhappy, anxious, and inferior-feeling individuals are deemed more "neurotic". A classic example of "neurotic" behavior is the panic attack. The Myers-Briggs Type Indicator personality types also somewhat correlate with the four temperaments. The test measures introversion/extroversion, but not emotional stability/instability (Cattell, 2004). Remnants of the four humors doctrine also remain in modern colloquial English. For example, we may refer to someone as "being in a good humor" when they are in a good mood.

Multi-Element Rites

The following rites involve more than one element and revolve around themes of harmony, health, and life balance. They have been performed numerous times and yielded decent results. See Appendix C for details.

Elemental Balancing Rite

Each of us has a unique elemental constitution that influences our health and personality. Thus, under this model, the route to health, harmony, and life balance will not be identical among individuals. This rite draws from your previous elemental work and serves as a general method to balance your inner elements.

Materials:
You will need your four elemental tools.

Preparation:
Place your earth tool in the north, your air tool in the east,

water tool in the west, and fire tool in the south. You will be walking around in a circle and drawing pentagrams, so make sure you have enough room.

Statement of Intent:
It is my will to balance my inner elements.

Procedure:
1. Face east, standing behind your air tool. Take a deep breath and center yourself. Pick up your air tool and draw an invoking air pentagram with it while cheerfully saying, *"XIQUAL DIJOW!"* [Ouranian Barbaric: Manifest air!] Smile and wave at the element as if to greet it. Take note of any physical sensations you feel, particularly focusing on those conveyed through your sense of smell. Set your air tool down in front of you.
2. Walk south, drawing a quarter circle from your pentagram (about chest height) until you arrive behind your fire tool. Face south and pick it up. Draw an invoking fire pentagram with it while shouting, *"XIQUAL ASHARA!"* [Manifest fire!] Take note of any physical sensations you feel, particularly focusing on those conveyed through your sense of sight. Also take note of any creative ideas or inspiration you receive. Set your fire tool down in front of you.
3. Walk west, drawing a quarter circle from your pentagram until you arrive behind your water tool. Face west and pick it up. Draw an invoking water pentagram with it while saying, *"XIQUAL THALDOMA!"* [Manifest water!] in your inner (astral) voice. Take note of any physical sensations you feel, particularly focusing on those conveyed through your sense of taste. Also take note of any intuitive messages you receive. Set your water tool down in front of you.

4. Walk north, drawing a quarter circle from your pentagram until you arrive behind your earth tool. Face north and pick it up. Draw an invoking earth pentagram with it while whispering, "*XIQUAL NOBO!*" [Manifest earth!] Knock on the ground to greet the element as if you are knocking on a door. Take note of any physical sensations you feel, particularly focusing on those conveyed through your sense of touch. Set your earth tool down in front of you.

5. Walk east, drawing a quarter circle from your pentagram until you reach the first pentagram you drew in the east. Your circle is now complete.

6. Walk into the center of your circle. Observe the pentagrams you drew with all five of your senses. Draw circles above you and below you while singing or chanting, "*XIQUAL MEWZHIQUAL!*" [Manifest aether!] Outstretch your hands and chant:

Fire burns, water churns,
Air carries, earth buries.
As above, so below.
Aether within me, blaze and glow!
Grant me balance, harmony, health,
and good fortune!
Elevate the opposite, refine the distortions!

7. Repeatedly chant the last line for as long as necessary. You will eventually feel well-balanced and refreshed.

Banishing:
Banish with laughter.

Love and Strife

Empedocles proposed the four "roots" exist together in various combinations, mixed by the motive forces of love and strife (in Simplicius, 158.1-159.4 [lines 1-35] + Strasbourg Papyrus *ensemble* a [lines 26-69] = DK 31B17 + Strasbourg Papyrus, *ensemble* a, trans. 2011). In his cosmology, "love" [Gk. φιλία] is a force of attraction and combination, while "strife" [νεῖκος] is a force of repulsion and separation. These two forces are engaged in a constant battle for domination of the universe, with each prevailing in turn in an endless cycle.

Here, you will channel these motive forces to balance the elements in eight parts of your psyche. Each part corresponds to one ray of the chaos star (Figure 6.2). Together, these "selves" comprise the totality of your being. The different "selves" you will interact with are: magical/pure self (octarine); war self (red); intellectual self (orange); sex self (purple or silver); ego self (yellow); love self (green); wealth self (blue); and death self (black).

Figure 6.2. The chaos star. In the chaos model, magic is classified according to function, with each represented by a different color. Octarine is the color of pure magic – everyone perceives it differently. Each ray further corresponds to one of the "selves" we harbor. Together, they compose our complete being. (Carroll, 1992)

Statement of Intent:
It is my will to achieve a state of perfect elemental harmony.

Procedure:
1. Take a deep breath and center yourself. Visualize yourself standing on top of a small, two-dimensional chaos star. It is small enough for your feet to completely cover. With each breath the star pulsates, expanding until it is a few meters in diameter.
2. To channel the motive force of strife, recite:

   Hail Eris, goddess of strife!
   Hail Azathoth, the nuclear chaos!
   I will to command the motive force
   that divides, disconnects from the darkest
   depths!
   Strife, discord, chaos, disharmony, dissonance,
   from the spaces in between the spaces,
   I invoke you!
   Hail Discordia, goddess of strife!
   Hail Satan, the great opposer!
   I will to shut out the order around me
   and channel the chaos inside!

3. Use the motive force of strife to separate your "selves" from each other. Visualize them walking towards their corresponding points on the chaos star, connected to you by an umbilical cord. As they face you, see each "self" glowing the appropriate color.
4. Observe how your "selves" interact with each other. Are any in conflict? Do any dominate the others? Do any look sad? Talk with the "selves" one by one. Use the motive force of strife to separate

any imbalances, remove negative energies, and do anything else you deem necessary.

5. After you are finished interacting with them, channel the motive force of love. Recite:

Hail Harmonia, goddess of concord!
Hail Amon-Gorloth, creator of cosmic equilibrium!
I will to command the motive force
that unites, amalgamates from the highest heavens!
Love, concord, order, harmony, congruence,
from the spaces in between the spaces,
I invoke you!
Hail Concordia, goddess of agreement!
Hail Jesus, prince of peace!
I will to channel the order around me
and conquer the chaos inside!

6. Again, talk with your "selves" one by one. Use the motive force of love to harmonize energies, seal gaps, and do anything else you deem necessary.
7. After you are finished interacting with your "selves," visualize them walking towards the center of the chaos star. As they merge back into you, the different colored lights merge, so you glow like a rainbow. The light slowly condenses in the center of your chest and then disappears.
8. Open your eyes and become reacquainted with your surroundings.

Banishing:
No banishing is required. Banishing with laughter is optional.

Baba Yaga Chicken Dance

Baba Yaga is the formidable witch with iron teeth in Russian folklore. She is most commonly depicted as an old woman with a long nose. She looks old, but nobody has any idea as to her actual age. To further confuse people, she can appear as three different women or look as young and pretty as she pleases. Despite her ferocious appetite, she's super skinny. Her favorite snacks are people who don't finish her chores, visitors knocking on her hut door that incorrectly answer her questions, and other assorted living creatures that piss her off. She also frequently kidnaps children and threatens to eat them.

Her forest hut is one-of-a-kind. The windows, when present, serve as eyes. A fence of bones to keep out intruders sometimes surrounds it. The eyes of the skulls light up at night! The whole thing has a rooster head on top and can move around on oversized chicken legs. To make the door appear you have to say the phrase, "Turn your back to the forest, your front to me."

She's the wild witch of the east, and isn't good or evil. She glides or flies through the forest in a mortar and uses the pestle as a rudder. She covers her tracks with a silver broom. She is the dark lady of magic that rules over the elements, death, and transformation. She will not harm the "pure of heart."

Here, we will harness Baba Yaga's transformative power to replace a negative personality trait with a positive one. We will draw sigils on our hands and "chicken dance" to summon her hut. Then we will clap away our negative traits while pushing the positive one into ourselves. The gnosis is exhaustion from dancing and pain from clapping really hard.

Materials:
You will need markers and "The Chicken Dance" music.

Preparation:
Choose a negative personality trait you want to eliminate and then determine its opposite. Write or sigilize the negative trait on your projective hand (the one you write with), and its opposite (the positive trait) on your receptive hand.

Statement of Intent:
It is my will to replace a negative trait with a positive one.

Procedure:
Stand in an area with enough distance to safely "chicken dance." Say:

Baba Yaga! Baba Yaga!
I search for you in the birch forest.
I call forth your house
that stands on chicken feet
at the edge of the underworld!
Teach me the ways of releasing and binding,
strength and yielding,
living and dying!
Wild witch of the elements,
untamed and unapologetic,
I evoke you!
Turn your back to the forest,
your front to me!

Start the music. Perform the chicken dance. Visualize your positive trait entering your receptive hand and the negative trait leaving your projective hand when clapping. On the claps, chant "***WON ME MORF-SNART***" until the song is over.

Banishing:
Banish with laughter.

Chapter 6 Homework

After taking notes on the chapter magical practice should be commenced for a minimum of 30 minutes each day for the remainder of the month. Perform the assignments in the order presented. Remember to document your efforts in your magical diary.

1. Meditate on the symbolism and arrangement of elements on the pentagram. What new insights into the pentagram and elemental forces can you discover?
2. Meditate on the elemental associations for each set of four. Then, "think in fours" to produce your own elemental correspondences. You may also rearrange any traditional associations to suit your personal practice if necessary.
3. Though the humoral explanation of disease was superseded, diet and exercise remain important contributors to our overall health. Determine what practical steps you can take to improve them, and then follow through. It is generally more effective to start with a few small changes and then work up to larger ones. If you are unsure where to start, consult with a licensed nutritionist or physician.
4. Analyze your soul mirrors – the lists of categorized traits you have compiled thus far. What overall elemental patterns are revealed? What relationships, if any, do your virtues and vices have with each other? Do you exhibit overbalance or underbalance of any elements?
5. Meditate on the mutability of the personality. Realize that you are totally awesome and totally messed up at the same time!
6. Perform the multi-element rites that facilitate harmony, health, and life balance sometime before moving on with your work. Feel free to modify them to your liking or substitute your own.

Chapter 7
Aether

So far, earth has provided our foundation, air has established a communicative basis, water has cultivated our intuition, and fire has provided the passion and willpower necessary to work with the elements. We have also gained insight into how the terrestrial elements interact with each other and work together. Our last stop among the classical western elements is aether, the transcendent element giving rise to the other four. The alchemical and *tattva* symbols for aether are shown in Figure 7.1. They are useful focal points in meditation and magical practice.

Figure 7.1. Common aether element symbols. The (a) alchemical symbols and (b) westernized *tattva* for elemental aether are shown. Aether has no single commonly accepted alchemical symbol, so two popular symbols are shown. The *tattvas* are Hindu in origin, but are occasionally used in western traditions. To make a colored image for your notes, color the *tattva* (inner egg) dark purple and its background (larger square) yellow.

The Western View of Aether

In the Greek model, aether is the fixed, unchanging quintessence that gave rise to the four terrestrial elements (Aristotle, *DC* 1.3, 270b1-26, trans. 2001). Aether lacks hot/cold and wet/dry characteristics and is instead associated with the celestial sphere and heavenly bodies. It does not move like the terrestrial elements under Aristotelian physics (*DC* 1.2, 268b15-16, 269a5-7, 269b1-6…, trans. 2001). Aether is the essence the Greek gods lived and breathed (Smith, 1862), is brighter and less dense than air (Plato, *Timaeus*, 58d), and is "subtler than light" (Fludd, 1659, p. 221). It was proposed to carry light waves and was a means to explain gravitation under Newtonian physics (cited in Schmiechen, 2009). Aether is not associated with a specific humor. Though the notion of an esoteric aether perpetuates in western culture, modern science has not found any empirical evidence supporting its existence (Lerner, 1996; Michelson & Morley, 1887).

In the Hermetic model aether also gives rise to the other four elements (Bardon, trans. 1956/2001). It is of a finer vibration than physical matter and "…connects these to the realms above and to the heavenly forms of the base elements" (Flowers, 1995, p. 67). It is the indefinable, incomprehensible primordial source and creative force known as the "All in All" or "God" (Bardon, trans. 1956/2001, p. 30). It is attributed to our "immortal spirit" and helps keep the terrestrial elements in equilibrium (pp. 50-52).

Complex Temperament Traits

You no doubt encountered virtues and vices that proved difficult to classify into one discrete elemental category during your introspection. These complex traits have roots in two or more elements. Further introspection and meditation will permit you to discover even more complex traits and underlying elemental components. One example of a complex trait is smoking cigarettes. Examples of how this trait may be broken down into individual elemental components are as follows:

Earth:
Some people smoke at certain times due to routine and force of habit. Some people may also smoke when they are bored or don't know what to do with their hands.

Air:
"Social smokers" smoke primarily around others, and rarely, if ever, smoke alone. It is often not a daily habit.

Water:
Smoking may be a coping mechanism to relieve nervousness, anxiety, or a host of other negative emotions.

Fire:
As with other forms of substance abuse, a predisposition towards addiction may compel some people to smoke. Underlying self-destructive urges may also be a factor.

***

People sharing the same complex trait may have completely different motivations, and thus underlying elemental influences. For example, my smoking is primarily a coping mechanism for anxiety and stress. The deep breathing calms me down, though meditation is more effective. Further, if I don't know what to do with my hands I will sometimes grab a cigarette without even thinking about it. In contrast, my best friend is primarily a social smoker, and rarely smokes alone. She has an addictive personality and smokes more frequently when she is in a self-destructive mood. She rarely, if ever, smokes due to nervousness or lack of being busy.

Western Aether Magic

In many western esoteric traditions aether is associated with religious, spiritual, illumination, transformation, unification, space-time, temple, and transcendental magic. In witchcraft it encompasses all directions, surpasses time and space, and is the turning wheel of the seasons (Starhawk, 1979/1999). Our sense of hearing and the colors black and white are also associated with elemental aether (Starhawk, 1979/1999). In witchcraft the aether element is represented by the cauldron (Starhawk, 1979/1999).

It is Lévi's Sphinx (trans. 1896/2001) with its Four Powers. Crowley (1944/2004) proposed "to go" as the emergent virtue of aether – it is "the token of Godhead" (p. 91). Deities traditionally associated with elemental aether include Asar (Egyptian), Iacchus (Greek), Liber (Roman), and Akasha (Hindu).

In ceremonial traditions the aether element is associated with the *Qabalistic* path connecting *Hod* [Splendor] and *Malkut* [Kingdom], which it shares with elemental fire (Crowley, 1909/1999). It is not associated with a *Qabalistic* world – it is more akin to the "negative veils" which emanated the *Tree of Life* instead. It has no Tetragrammaton letter, but is the ש of the Pentagrammaton, the five-letter reconstructed name of Jesus (Crowley, 1909/1999). Aether transcends masculine/feminine, active/passive, and other dichotomies attributed to the terrestrial elements. Its *Qabalistic* King scale color is white merging into gray (Crowley, 1909/1999). Dark purple is also associated with elemental aether (Bardon, trans. 1956/2001). It is not attributed to a traditional ceremonial tool (Crowley, 1909/1999), but I have seen some magicians assign the lamp to aether instead of fire.

In contrast to the terrestrial elements, aether lacks a thorough "top-down" Hebrew hierarchy. Its divine name in ʾAṣilut is יהשוה [Heb. *YHShWH*], the Pentagrammaton and five-letter reconstructed name of Jesus (Crowley, 1909/1999). No archangel, choir of angels, angel, elemental ruler, elemental king, or elementals are traditionally assigned to elemental aether. In some witchcraft and ceremonial traditions I have seen magicians attribute מטטרון [Heb. *Meṭaṭron*] to aether. This high-ranking angel appears only in Jewish literature, bears the Tetragrammaton, and serves as the voice of *YHWH* (Jacobs & Blau, 1906).

Thinking in Fives

There are several sets of five present in nature. There are five senses, fingers of the human hand, and more. There are also many sets of five present in western culture. Many of these "fives" hold magical significance – each member of a set reflects the qualities of a specific element, with all five elements being ultimately represented. This is how magical correspondences are produced. Traditional western magical correspondences for each element are shown in Table 7.1.

Table 7.1. *Traditional Western Magical Correspondences of the Five Elements*

Attribute	Earth	Air	Water	Fire	Aether
Sense[a]	Touch	Smell	Taste	Sight	Hearing
Human finger[b]	Middle	Little	Index	Ring	Thumb
Aspect of the spirit[c]	Consciousness	Intellect	Feelings	Will	Conscience
Tetramorph[d]	Bull	Man	Eagle	Lion	Sphinx

Information is adapted from [a]Starhawk (1979/1999), [b]Buckland (2004), Cherubim (2004), [c]Bardon (trans. 1959/2001), and [d]Crowley (1909/1999). Note that alternate correspondence schemes with equally valid rationales exist.

Correspondences such as these are commonly used to enhance magical work. You may incorporate as many or as few of them into your practice as you'd like. The ability to "think in fives" will permit you to produce your own personally significant elemental correspondences. What other fives in nature or western culture can you think of? Which element would you assign to each member of a set and why? Example rationales justifying the correspondences in Table 7.1 are as follows:

Senses:
Traditional correspondences for the senses reflect how we perceive our surroundings in a manner consistent with each element's nature. In witchcraft the senses of touch, smell, taste, sight, and hearing correspond to the elements of earth, air, water, fire, and aether, respectively (Starhawk, 1979/1999). However, note that alternate correspondence schemes with equally valid rationales exist (see Bardon, trans. 1956/2001).

Our sense of touch provides us with valuable physical data about the world around us. This reflects elemental earth, the most physical and tactile element. Our sense of smell allows us to detect odors that may carry important messages. This reflects elemental air, the most mobile and communicative element. Water is the most absorptive element. Our sense of taste could not function without water, as our tongue needs to be wet to detect flavors. Fire is the brightest element. Our sense of sight could not function without light, an aspect of fire. Aether is the transcendent element. Our sense of hearing reflects its nature, as sound is borne through vibrations. Vibrations are the foundation of the creation of the universe in many paradigms.

Human Fingers:
The five fingers of the human hand are linked to the elements in many paradigms (see Altman, 2009). In witchcraft (Buckland, 2004) and ceremonial magic (Cherubim, 2004) the middle finger, little, index finger, ring finger, and thumb traditionally correspond to elemental earth, air, water, fire, and aether, respectively. However, note that alternate correspondence schemes with equally valid rationales exist (see Bardon, trans.

1956/2001). Hermetic correspondences are consistent with Hinduism.

The traditional correspondences of the fingers somewhat correlate with their divinatory implications in western palmistry (see Altman, 2009; Buckland, 2004). Our middle finger relates to our propriety, responsibility, and other earth-associated traits. Our little finger relates to our intellect, communication, thought process, and other air-associated traits. Our index finger relates to our leadership, ambition, and drive to succeed. Note that the index finger is traditionally associated with elemental water, but these traits are often associated with elemental fire. Our ring finger relates to our creativity and self-expression. Note that the ring finger is traditionally associated with elemental fire, but these traits are often associated with elemental fire or water. Our thumb relates to our energy level, life force, and other traits traditionally associated with fire or aether.

Aspects of the Spirit:
Hermetic philosophy links each aspect of the spirit to a particular element (Bardon, trans. 1956/2001). Our conscience emerges from the interactions of consciousness (earth), intellect (air), feelings (water), and will (fire). Aether is an appropriate correspondence, as our conscience emerges from these aspects working together. Other paradigms attribute the elements to aspects of our spirit in a similar manner (see Conway, 2005; Crowley, 1909/1999; Starhawk, 1979/1999; Wolfe, 1998).

Tetramorphs:
The four kerubic creatures described in Ezekiel's vision (Ezekiel 10:14, *King James Bible*) were likely influenced by Assyrian culture (Whittick, 1960). The different animal heads of these tetramorphs bear connection with the four fixed signs of the zodiac, which in turn relate back to the

elements (Crowley, 1909/1999). Taurus (the bull) corresponds to elemental earth, Aquarius (the water bearer) to air, Scorpio (the scorpion) to water, and Leo (the lion) to fire. The eagle has long been an alternate symbol for Scorpio, emphasizing its spiritual nature (Hall, 1928). The sphinx is a chimera of these four animals, and is recognized as a symbol of aether in both witchcraft (Starhawk, 1979/1999) and ceremonial magic (Crowley, 1909/1999).

Aether in Chaos Magic

The aether element may be applied to magical practice in numerous ways. Various egregores, godforms, or pop culture characters associated with elemental aether may be invoked or evoked. Divination may be practiced via interpreting sounds. Enchantment may be performed for space-time, integrative, and personal transformation purposes. All illumination work is broadly associated with aether. Working with aether tends to be highly personal, so it is challenging to make generalizations about it.

Aether transcends heavy/light, dark/bright, passive/active, and other dichotomies. It is divine essence. It is spirit. It carries the life force known by many names: the *pneúma* of the ancient Greeks (Strong, 1982a, #4151), the *ruaḥ* of the Hebrews (Strong, 1982b, #7308), the *prāṇa* of the Hindus (*Chāndogya Upaniṣad*, trans. 1996), the *mana* of the Melanesians (Codrington, 1891), and the *qì* of the Chinese (Maciocia, 2015; Wen, 2016). In chaos magic the sum of all life may be personified as Lévi's Baphomet, as described in the *Mass of Chaos B* (Carroll, 1987):

In the first aeon, I was the Great Spirit.
In the second aeon, Men knew me as The Horned God, Pangenitor Panphage.
In the third aeon, I was the Dark one, the Devil.

In the fourth aeon, Men knew me not,
for I am the Hidden One.
In this new aeon, I appear before you as Baphomet
The God before all gods,
who shall endure to the end of the Earth. (pp. 131-132)

These characteristics have been incorporated into the aether rites, which are intentionally integrative and open-ended. Many incorporate a gnosis through sound concentration to be consistent with the elemental theme. Some also use the invoking and banishing elemental pentagrams (Figure 7.2). It is best to commit them to memory.

invoking spirit   banishing spirit
(active)   (active)

invoking spirit   banishing spirit
(passive)   (passive)

Figure 7.2. Elemental aether (spirit) invoking and banishing pentagrams. Draw the pentagrams with your magical tool or finger. Begin at the dot and continue drawing in the direction of the arrow. When you arrive back at the dot, your pentagram is complete.

The aether (spirit) pentagrams integrate the other elements and may be "active" or "passive" in nature. Active pentagrams allow you to implant quintessence, whereas passive pentagrams permit submissive reception of it. Invoking pentagrams facilitate an integrated point of view, whereas banishing pentagrams disconnect you from it. The active invoking pentagram follows the terrestrial elements in order of increasing density (i.e., fire, air, water, earth), with aether as the last element in the sequence. The passive invoking pentagram follows the elements in order of decreasing density (i.e., earth, water, air, fire, aether).

Drawing the pentagrams is generally more effective when one has already achieved some degree of elemental balance. It is worth drawing each one separately to investigate their individual effects; however, the passive invoking pentagram should be used carefully – it can make you unresistingly receptive to anything and everything. After investigating the passive invoking pentagram, draw a passive banishing one to cancel it out. Looking across paradigms, the spirit pentagrams are not frequently used in rituals. Thus, rites that incorporate each one are intentionally included so you can gain some experience working with them.

Attuning with Aether

Obtain a small bell, tuning fork, or other instrument that produces a pleasant, long tone. Take a deep breath, center yourself, and ring it. Focus your attention on the sound. Observe a moment of silence after the sound dissipates. With each successive ring, we will focus on how our senses respond to the sound. By the end of the exercise, all five of your senses will be working in harmony.

1. Ring it again, focusing on your sense of touch. Physically feel the sound waves hitting your skin and vibrating the fluid in your ears. Observe a moment of silence after the sound dissipates.
2. Ring it again, additionally focusing on your sense of smell. Inhale deeply to smell the changes in the air produced by the tone. Observe a moment of silence after the sound dissipates.
3. Ring it again, additionally focusing on your sense of taste. Stick out your tongue to taste the vibrations produced by the tone. Observe a moment of silence after the sound dissipates.
4. Ring it again, additionally focusing on your sense of sight. Visualize the sound waves in the air. What

do they look like? How quickly are they moving? Are they homogenous, or do the sound waves change when they hit different objects? Observe a moment of silence after the sound dissipates.

5. Ring it again. Observe the tone using all five of your senses simultaneously. Continue until all five of your senses are working in harmony observing the tone.

Aether Entrance Rite

Materials:
You will need your attuning tool. This will become your elemental aether tool unless the universe has other plans for you.

Statement of Intent:
It is my will to access elemental aether.

Procedure:
Find a quiet area and sit in a comfortable position with your attuning tool. Attune with elemental aether. Take your time and do not rush.

Draw an active invoking spirit pentagram with your instrument. Observe it with all five of your senses. Say, *"FACH FIACOPA!"* [Ouranian Barbaric: I penetrate the aether!] Observe the vibrations your voice produces. Chant the following and vibrate the Hebrew names:

Quintessence, in the name of *YHShWH* I greet you! Grant me access to elemental aether. Integrative, divine, transcendental, sublime, may its celestial light descend and bring spirit to earth!

Take note of any physical sensations you feel, particularly focusing on those conveyed through your sense of hearing. Also take note of anything nonphysical you perceive.

Draw a triangle around your pentagram. Observe it with all five of your senses. Chant the following and vibrate the Hebrew names:

Meṭaṭron, Chancellor of Heaven, in the name of YHShWH I evoke you! Grant me access to elemental aether. Breathe life into this tool so I may further integrate with it!

If you do not sense *Meṭaṭron's* presence, repeatedly chant his name until you do. After you are finished communicating with him, thank him and send him on his way.

Banishing:
Banish with laughter.

Invoking Active Spirit: A Pathworking

In the previous chapter you took concrete steps to balance your inner elements. Here, we will integrate them through pathworking. A pathworking is a journey that takes place in the mind's eye through a series of guided visualizations. They are present in many western esoteric traditions and have a profound impact on the consciousness. They also provide opportunities to more deeply investigate the underlying symbolism of the universe. Some paths are well tread, and others not so much.

Procedure:
Find a quiet area and sit in a comfortable position. Close your eyes. Take a deep breath and center yourself. With each breath, you feel calmer and more relaxed. Feel the tension in your toes. As you exhale, this tension dissipates until they are completely relaxed. As you continue to breathe your relaxation grows, spreading through the tops and bottoms of your feet into your ankles. They are now

completely relaxed. It continues, travelling up your legs and into your knees, which are now completely relaxed. Feel the lack of tension in your shins and calves. Any outside noises or distractions just serve to relax you further. Now your upper legs, hips, and pelvis are completely relaxed. As you continue to breathe, your waist, chest, and back are completely relaxed. Your relaxation grows further, moving into your shoulders, then down into your arms, hands, and fingers. Everything below your neck is now completely relaxed. The relaxation expands as you breathe, filling your neck and face. Feel your chin, jaw, nose, cheeks, eyes, eyelids, forehead, and ears relax. Finally, feel your scalp relax. Your entire body is now completely relaxed.

In your mind's eye, draw an active invoking pentagram. It glows a brilliant white. Observe it with all of your five senses. See its brightness, smell its cleanliness, taste its purity, and touch its warmth. Does it emanate a sound? The pentagram slowly dissolves, revealing a dark purple egg. It is a few meters taller than you are and emanates an unwavering calmness. As you touch the egg to investigate, you feel that it is not solid – it is composed of a dark purple liquid. The liquid soothes you as you touch it and is cool but not uncomfortable.

You step through the egg. On the other side you are greeted by an expansive blackness that reminds you of outer space. As your eyes adjust, you realize you are in a large black room. There are four doors on the far wall. Your footsteps echo on the floor as you move towards them. Each door is painted with a westernized *tattva* belonging to one of the four terrestrial elements. The leftmost door corresponds to earth – there is a yellow square painted on a larger dark purple square. The next door corresponds to air – there is a light blue circle painted on an orange square. The third door corresponds to water – there is a white crescent painted on a black circle. The far right door corresponds to fire – there is a red triangle painted on a green square.

You walk over to the earth door and stand before it. You gaze at it for a few moments, mesmerized by the yellow square painted on the dark purple background. You take a deep breath, open the door, and step through.

You enter into a spacious cavern. You smell cool, dry air as you look around. It is completely silent. As your eyes adjust to the dim light, mighty rock walls come into focus. It feels as if they looking down, quietly observing you. Your eyes are drawn to a silhouette in the center of the cavern. As you move closer to investigate, you feel the steadiness of the ground below and smell the earthy richness of the air. The silhouette emits a protective vibration, its wings poised as if guarding the cavern. When you reach the cavern's center, you stand before the figure of an archangel. He holds a scroll in one hand and a burning flame in the other. You realize you are standing before 'Uri 'el, archangel of elemental earth. You may talk with 'Uri 'el for as long as you'd like. After you are finished, you thank him and head back through the cavern to the elemental door. Take a moment to process your experience before exiting the cavern.

You pass through the door and reorient yourself to the blackness of the first room. You walk over to the air door and stand before it. You gaze at it for a few moments, mesmerized by the light blue circle painted on the orange background. You take a deep breath, open the door, and step through.

You are on the summit of a high mountain. As you squint while your eyes adjust to the sunlight, you smell warm, wet air and hear birds chirping in the distance. Patches of vibrant green grass punctuate the rocky summit. It is springtime, so the atmosphere is lighthearted and cheerful. As you look around, your eyes are drawn to the silhouette of a winged figure perched on the highest rock.

Grass rustles beneath your feet as you move closer to investigate. As you climb, the sunny rocks warm your hands. As you make your way closer, the winged figure gazes out into the horizon, unaffected by your presence. You sit beside him for a moment and look out at the horizon, sharing a comfortable silence. There are clouds, birds, and other mountain peaks in the distance. You are sitting beside *Rafa'el*, archangel of elemental air. Like other archangels, he can assume any form he pleases. You may talk with *Rafa'el* for as long as you'd like, or sit quietly beside him and enjoy the silence. After you are finished, you thank him and head back down the rocks and through the grass to the elemental door. Take a moment to process your experience before exiting the mountain summit.

You pass through the door and reorient yourself to the blackness of the first room. You walk over to the water door and stand before it. You gaze at it for a few moments, mesmerized by the white crescent painted on the black circle. You take a deep breath, open the door, and step through.

You step onto a calm, quiet beach at twilight. Waves gently crash on the shore as you smell the ocean air. The full moon is softly glowing in the sky. Damp sand crunches beneath your feet as you make your way to the water's edge. In the distance your eyes are drawn to a winged silhouette illuminated by the moonlight. It silently looks out at the ocean, and you get the distinct feeling he or she is waiting for you. As you walk closer, the figure turns to meet your gaze. You are standing before *Gavri'el*, archangel of elemental water. He has an important message for you. You may talk with *Gavri'el* for as long as you'd like. After you are finished, you thank him and head back across the beach to the elemental door. Take a moment to process your experience before exiting the beach.

You pass through the door and reorient yourself to the blackness of the first room. You walk over to the fire door and stand before it. You gaze at it for a few moments, mesmerized by the red triangle painted on the green background. You take a deep breath, open the door, and step through.

The sweltering heat of volcanic ash immediately hits your face. The air smells hot and dry. As the ash settles you realize you are at the base of a great volcano that just erupted. Rivers of lava flow all around, glowing bright orange scarlet and emitting visible heat waves. As you look down, you see that patches of lava have cooled enough for you to step on. They appear to almost form a path. Intrigued, you follow the "path" as if you are hopping across stepping-stones. As you hop over the smaller pools of lava, you hear hotter lava sizzle as it oozes into cooler areas. As the ash settles more, you see the silhouette of a mighty archangel with outstretched wings. Faint war cries can be heard from the direction he is looking in. You hop over in his general direction to get a closer look. As you approach, he turns his head and begins walking toward you. Faint war cries can still be heard amidst a backdrop of sizzling lava. You are now face to face with *Mika'el*, archangel of elemental fire. He has been waiting to talk with you for a long time. You may talk with *Mika'el* for as long as you'd like. After you are finished, you thank him and head back down the "path" to the elemental door. Take a moment to process your experience before exiting the base of the volcano.

You pass through the door and reorient yourself to the blackness of the first room. As you slowly make your way back to the purple egg exit on the other side, your footsteps echo on the ground. Halfway to the exit, you pause and look back at the elemental doors one last time. As you realize that this room represents elemental aether, you feel as if you are being watched. *Metatron* is smiling down on you. As you continue walking back to the egg, he conveys that you can revisit the portals any time you wish, as you now know the way here. As you approach the dark purple egg, you feel more peaceful and balanced than before. The cool liquid of the egg soothes you as you touch it. You take a deep breath and then step through.

You have returned to the room where your physical body resides. You turn around to look at the dark purple egg one last time. Draw an active banishing pentagram in front of the egg. As your pentagram slowly dissipates, so does the egg. As the last bits of the pentagram and egg fade, you begin to feel your fingers and toes. You gradually feel the rest of your body. Slowly open your eyes and become reacquainted with your surroundings. Stand up when you are ready and document your experience in your magical diary.

Invoking Passive Spirit: Wholehearted Surrender

Preparation:
You may perform the Lesser Banishing Ritual of the Pentagram (see Appendix D) or some other general banishing beforehand to clear your space of any unnecessary junk. You may also perform any additional banishing you feel is necessary. Don't go overboard, as over-banishing can make it difficult to invoke desired energies into a space afterwards.

Choose an energy you are having trouble integrating into your life that you would like to wholeheartedly surrender to. "Christ Consciousness" and "Buddha Consciousness" are popular choices. Do not choose halfheartedly. After picking something, contemplate this energy deeply. Why are you having trouble integrating it into your life? Are there any potential caveats to wholehearted surrender? Are you prepared for the (sometimes jarring) removal of mental and emotional roadblocks necessary for its successful integration?

Statement of Intent:
It is my will to integrate [energy] into my life in a positive manner.

Procedure:
1. Sit in a comfortable position and meditate on the energy you want to unresistingly surrender to. Let it take form in your mind's eye.
2. Observe this energy carefully with all five of your senses. What does it look, taste, smell, and feel like? What does it sound like? Are your observations consistent with what you expected?
3. Communicate with this energy. Is its nature consistent with what you expected? If you have reservations, banish without proceeding further. Better safe than sorry!
4. When ready, draw a passive invoking pentagram. Feel this energy entering and integrating with you. Observe it with all five of your senses. Feel how it faces no opposition.
5. Visualize this energy integrating into all of your cells. Take note of any sensations you feel, particularly focusing on those conveyed through your five senses. Take your time and do not rush.
6. Anchor this integrated state to a word, sound, gesture, or something else. That way, you can call on it when needed in the future.

Banishing:
Banish with laughter while drawing a passive banishing pentagram.

Aether Element Monasticism

This monasticism serves to further integrate you with elemental aether. The monasticism should be performed for five days or five weeks, since this number is associated with the quintessence. However, feel free to use another aether-related number if it suits your fancy. Carry your aether tool at all times during the monasticism – this serves as a constant reminder of elemental aether and increases vigilance. After your monasticism is complete, keep your aether tool someplace special, such as an altar or favorite shelf in your study area. You may use your tool for future aether workings and reuse it if you perform the monasticism again. The Lesser Observances are accomplishable for someone who regularly has a busy schedule. The Extreme Observances are intended for someone who has extended free time. The Greater Observances are a mean between the two. The overall monasticism format is inspired by Peter J. Carroll (1992, pp. 187-90).

Beginning the Monasticism:
Find a quiet area and sit in a comfortable position with your attuning tool. Attune with elemental aether. Take your time and do not rush.

Draw an active invoking spirit pentagram with your instrument. Observe the pentagram with all five of your senses. Say, *"FACH FIACOPA!"* [Ouranian Barbaric: I penetrate the aether!] Observe the vibrations your voice produces. Chant the following and vibrate the Hebrew names:

Quintessence, in the name of *YHShWH* I greet you! It is my will to perform the [Lesser/Greater/Extreme] Observances of Aether for five [days/weeks]. May this monasticism further integrate us and may *Meṭaṭron* watch over me!

Lesser Observances:
1. Carry your aether tool at all times. If you can't carry it openly keep it in your pocket or a bag and carry that with you.

2. Develop and perform a simple daily activity to connect with elemental aether.
3. Perform a simple aether element rite that incorporates your tool each day.
4. Meditate on the concepts of transcendence or "life force" each day.
5. Dedicate any sound concentration gnosis to elemental aether.

Greater Observances:
1. Perform all of the Lesser Observances.
2. Perform a second daily aether element rite that incorporates your tool.
3. Relate all of your daily meditation and magical work to elemental aether. Include it however you see fit.
4. Explore which archetypal forces recur across paradigms. Compare and contrast how they are perceived and represented. If you are unsure where to begin *Interfaith Online* (http://www.Interfaith. org/), *Internet Sacred Text Archive* (http://www. sacred-texts.com/), and *Encyclopedia Mythica* (http://www.pantheon.org/) are starting places.

Extreme Observances:
1. Perform all of the Greater Observances.
2. Perform a third daily aether element rite that incorporates your tool.
3. In the spirit of *The Dice Man* by Luke Rhinehart, randomly shift to a different paradigm each day. Obtain a six-sided die and assign each side to a paradigm you explored during the Greater Observances. Roll the die each morning upon waking and fully live in that paradigm for the entire day. All magical operations should also be consistent with the paradigm. Alternatively, you may use the paradigm scheme presented in *Liber Null &*

Psychonaut (Carroll, 1987, pp. 72-75). If you perform this exercise long enough everything will seem the same, and the system underlying the system will reveal itself.

Concluding the Monasticism:

Return to the place you began your monasticism. Attune with elemental aether. Take your time and do not rush.

Draw an active invoking spirit pentagram with your instrument. Observe the pentagram with all five of your senses. Chant:

Quintessence, I greet you! I willed to perform the [Lesser/Greater/Extreme] Observances of Aether for five [days/weeks]. May my past, present, and future actions connect us beyond time and space!

Chapter 7 Homework

After taking notes on the chapter magical practice should be commenced for a minimum of 30 minutes each day for the remainder of the month. Perform the assignments in the order presented. Remember to document your efforts in your magical diary.

1. Meditate on the topic of elemental aether for a minimum of 10 minutes each day. How does it affect your life? How do you interact with it?
2. Identify the elemental components underlying your complex traits. Categorize each trait as having extreme, moderate, or little influence in your daily life. You may also perform introspection to discover additional complex traits, or revise classifications of previous traits if necessary. Update your magical diary as needed.
3. Meditate on the elemental associations for each set of

five. Then, "think in fives" to produce your own elemental correspondences. You may also rearrange any traditional associations to suit your personal practice if necessary.

4. Investigate the effects of the four aether pentagrams. Remember to draw a passive banishing pentagram after investigating the passive invoking pentagram to cancel it out. Otherwise, you will walk around unresistingly open to everything.

5. Attune with elemental aether at least once daily for a period of one week.

6. Perform the entrance rite. After obtaining your aether tool purify and consecrate it by infusing it with divine vibrations in whatever manner you see fit.

7. Perform the aether element invocation rites at least once during the month. Feel free to modify them to your liking or substitute your own.

8. Perform an aether element monasticism before concluding work with this element.

Chapter 8
Buddhist Elements

Differences among western and eastern thinking are often overemphasized. Human cultures throughout time have pursued truth, beauty, and goodness, though their approaches may differ. Historically, ancient Greek (especially Socratic) philosophy permeated western thinking and value systems. Society emphasizes the role of the individual and individual rights. Priority is often placed on personal opinion and finding an absolute truth. Historically, ancient Indian (e.g., Hindu, Buddhist) and Chinese philosophy permeated eastern thinking and value systems. Society emphasizes harmony, balance, and social responsibility. Priority is not placed on personal opinion and finding an absolute truth. Globalization and modern technology are further blurring the divides between these thinking modalities.

So far we have explored the western elements, internalized them, and determined how they impact our lives. We have also magically interacted with them and harnessed them to achieve harmony, health, and life balance. Here, we will explore the eastern elements. Eastern cosmology shares some major themes with western cosmology, but there are significant differences. Thus, the elements and magic as a whole are approached in a different manner. Major eastern models relevant to our elemental work are Buddhism and ancient Chinese philosophy. We will begin our exploration with Buddhism. Symbols for the five Buddhist elements are shown in Figure 8.1. They are useful focal points in meditation and magical practice.

| earth | water | fire | air | space |

Figure 8.1. Common Buddhist element symbols. To make a colored image for your notes, traditional color correspondences and shapes are as follows: earth, yellow square; water, blue circle; fire, red triangle; air, green semicircle or crescent; and space, white drop (Beer, 2003). This color scheme is consistent with the one presented in *The Tibetan Book of the Dead* (Thurman (Trans.), 1994). In some traditions blue and white are switched (Beer, 2003).

The Buddhist Paradigm

Buddhism originated in northern India around 500 BCE, and is based on the teachings of Siddhartha Gautama, the historical Buddha (Skilton, 1994/2001). He was born to affluent parents, and the story goes that a seer prophesized the infant would become a great political or spiritual figure. His parents ensured his childhood years were joyful and carefree. As a teenager, his curiosity toward the outside world put an end to his sheltered life. When he first witnessed pain and suffering it impacted him deeply, sparking a lifelong quest for truth and liberation. He abandoned his life of luxury and travelled in search of teachers that could provide guidance. He ultimately pursued an ascetic lifestyle, gaining powerful insight into the human condition. His final words were, "All compounded things are liable to decay; strive with mindfulness" (quoted in Skilton, 1994/2001, p. 24).

From India, Buddhism spread across the globe and is present in many societies today. Its primary sacred texts are the *sūtras* [San. threads] containing the original words and teachings of the historical Buddha. In the Pali language they are called *suttas*. Discussing them in great detail is beyond the scope of this workbook, but additional information and recommended reading, should you choose to pursue it, are available at *The Buddhist Society* (http://www.thebuddhist society.org/), *Buddhanet* (http://www.buddhanet.net), and *His Holiness the 14th Dalai Lama of Tibet* (http://www.dalailama.com). If you prefer print resources, works by Robert Thurman or B. Alan Wallace are highly recommended. Fundamental concepts and principles that will enhance your work with the Buddhist elements are as follows:

Reincarnation:
Impermanence is considered an absolute truth in Buddhism (Skilton, 1994/2001). The concept of an eternal, unchanging soul is absent. Our thoughts, feelings, and perceptions change as we experience new things. When we die this energy is reestablished in a new body. The birth-death cycle perpetuates until *nirvāṇa*, the highest liberated state of enlightenment, is reached. His Holiness the 14th Dalai Lama of Tibet (2011) states, "There are two ways in which someone can take rebirth after death: rebirth under the sway of karma and destructive emotions and rebirth through the power of compassion and prayer" (par. 13).

Some say there no intermediate state between death and rebirth (McClelland, 2010), while others say there is (Thurman (Trans.), 1994). Some say rebirth occurs immediately (McClelland, 2010), while others say it takes up to 49 days (Thurman (Trans.), 1994). The earliest stages of death bear direct elemental significance – death begins with the ordered dissolution of elements in the gross body (Bhattacharyya, 1980; Thurman (Trans.), 1994).

Karma:
Concepts of moral causation were present in India well before the advent of Buddhism (Trainor, 2004; Williams, Tribe, & Wynne, 2000/2012). The *karma* (intention and actions) of the previous life determines the circumstances

of rebirth. His Holiness the 14th Dalai Lama of Tibet (2011) states:

> *...due to ignorance negative and positive karma are created and their imprints remain on the consciousness. These are reactivated through craving and grasping, propelling us into the next life. We then take rebirth involuntarily in higher or lower realms. This is the way ordinary beings circle incessantly through existence like the turning of a wheel. Even under such circumstances ordinary beings can engage diligently with a positive aspiration in virtuous practices in their day-to-day lives. They familiarise themselves with virtue that at the time of death can be reactivated providing the means for them to take rebirth in a higher realm of existence. On the other hand, superior Bodhisattvas, who have attained the path of seeing, are not reborn through the force of their karma and destructive emotions, but due to the power of their compassion for sentient beings and based on their prayers to benefit others. They are able to choose their place and time of birth as well as their future parents. Such a rebirth, which is solely for the benefit of others, is rebirth through the force of compassion and prayer.* (par. 13)

The "poisons" (non-virtuous mental states) and "wisdoms" (virtuous mental states) underpinning our *karma* bear connection with the elements. Five elemental Buddhas can transmute these poisons into wisdoms (discussed in Thurman (Trans.), 1994). Different realms of rebirth are associated with different poisons.

Realms of Rebirth:
The *karma* accumulated in life dictates the realm of rebirth. Virtuous *karma* lands you in a higher realm, whereas non-virtuous *karma* lands you in a lower realm. The five realms in Theravada Buddhist cosmology are listed in the *Mahasihanada Sutta* (MN 12; Thera & Bodhi (Trans.), 1994). Some

The Elemental Magic Workbook

of the realms mirror Hindu cosmology (see *The Garuda Purana* (Wood & Subrahmanyam (Trans.), 1911)). The five realms, listed in descending order, are:

Deva Realm: Rebirth as a *deva* [San. god] results from virtuous *karma*. They are more powerful, longer-lived, and generally happier than humans. They don't have to work, but may grow lazy or overly attached to things. Here, they are vulnerable to the poison of pride (Thurman (Trans.), 1994). Virtuous people such as Mahatma Gandhi and Saint Teresa of Calcutta ("Mother Teresa") were probably reborn here.

Human Realm: Rebirth as a human is rare and advantageous (*Pansu Suttas: Dust*, SN 56.102-113; Bhikkhu (Trans.), 2011). Humans have a unique capacity for ethics and an opportunity to directly reach *nirvāṇa*. Thus, Buddhas are always human. Humans experience a wide range of pleasure and pain. Here they may suffer from all five poisons, but are free from the quantities of delusion, lust, and hate that bind beings in the lower realms (Thurman (Trans.), 1994). You are here.

Animal Realm: Rebirth as an animal is less advantageous than rebirth as a *deva* or human. Wild animals may be attacked or killed and often live in fear. Lacking the security and comfort of higher realms, they also run the risk of enslavement. Here, they suffer from the poison of delusion (Thurman (Trans.), 1994). Your pets live here.

Preta Realm: Rebirth as a *preta* [San. ghost] results from non-virtuous *karma*. They suffer from excess cravings and attachments (Thurman (Trans.), 1994). Constantly yearning for more, they are never satisfied with what they have. The famed "hungry ghosts" are often depicted with small mouths and huge stomachs to reflect this. Here, they suffer from the poison of lust (Thurman (Trans.), 1994). They may be reborn into a higher realm when their non-virtuous *karma* has been depleted. My narcissistic, shallow, thieving, materialistic ex will probably be reborn here.

Naraka *Realm:* Rebirth as a denizen of *naraka* [San. hells] results from considerable non-virtuous *karma*. The worst offenders are reborn here. Duration and nature of punishment is proportional to the quantity of bad *karma* accumulated. The *Bala-pandita Sutta* (MN 129) and *Devaduta Sutta* (MN 130) graphically describe how unpleasant the realm is. Here, its denizens suffer from the poison of hate (Thurman (Trans.), 1994). They may be reborn into a higher realm when their non-virtuous *karma* has been depleted. Adolf Hitler and Joseph Stalin were probably reborn here.

***

The highest two realms (*deva*, human) are considered desirable, whereas the lower three (animal, *preta*, *naraka*) are not. In some traditions six destinations are acknowledged instead of five. The sixth destination is the home of the *ásura* [San. demigods/titans], located between the *deva* and human realms. They are jealous gods who suffer from the poison of envy (Thurman (Trans.), 1994). In earlier holy texts the *deva* and *ásura* are not subdivided into separate realms.

Buddhist Magic

The historical Buddha did not have a high opinion of magic and fortunetelling. Despite this, esoteric Buddhism developed a rich magical tradition under the backdrop of Hinduism (Bhattacharyya, 1980). Older Tibetan grimoires and medical texts also suggest a shamanic influence (see Gouin, 2010; Lindahl, 2010). Some key Buddhist practices relevant to our elemental work are:

Mantras:

A *mantra* is a sacred sound intoned for invocation, evocation, illumination, protection, raising energy, and more. It may be whispered, hummed, or spoken normally, either aloud or in the mind's eye. Repetitions are typically counted on a string of prayer beads. Each elemental Buddha is associated with a particular seed syllable (Beer, 2003). A seed syllable is a single syllable *mantra* containing the essence of that Buddha (Thurman (Trans.), 1994).

Mudrās:

A *mudrā* [San. seal] is a symbolic hand gesture that directs energies and connects us to specific concepts. It may involve the right, left, or both hands. Some involve holding sacred objects. Each elemental Buddha is associated with a particular *mudrā* (Bhattacharyya, 1980).

Āsanas:

An *āsana* [San. seat] is a physical posture connected with yoga. When performing an *āsana* you should feel comfortable and stable, but also observe your mental and physical reactions to the postures. You may sit in a particular *āsana* when performing *mantras* or *mudrās*.

Maṇḍalas:

A *maṇḍala* [San. circle] is a symbolic depiction of the universe. In some traditions *maṇḍalas* serve as meditation aids or symbolic offerings. Tibetan sand paintings feature stunning *maṇḍalas*, which are valuable teaching tools to convey various wisdoms and the concept of impermanence. More information on sand *maṇḍalas*, should you choose to pursue it, is available at *LOSANG SAMTEN* (http://www.losangsamten.com/mandalas.html) and *Namygal Monastery* (http://www.namgyal.org/sand-mandalas/).

Buddhist Model of the Elements

The Buddhist elements were introduced late enough that Hindu and Greek influence cannot be ruled out. The four "great elements" described in the *Maha-hatthipadopama Sutta* (MN 28; Bhikkhu (Trans.), 2003) are earth, water, fire, and wind, which manifest as solidity, fluidity, heat (energy), and movement, respectively. Sometimes "air" is called "wind" to emphasize its mobile nature. The elements cannot exist without perception. The question "If a tree falls in a forest and no one is around to hear it, does it make a sound?" illustrates the concept of observable reality. The tree produces vibrations when it falls and hits the ground. If no ears hear the vibrations, they will remain undetected.

Purification of the elemental aggregates is a basis of liberation from the cycle of death and rebirth. The aggregates work together to form personal experience, and each elemental Buddha embodies an aggregate (discussed in Thurman (Trans.), 1994). The elemental Buddhas are applicable to Buddhist psychology and may represent mental constructs or emotions. Each one is associated with a particular aggregate, poison, wisdom, seed syllable, *mudrā*, and more. Their placement in the context of the five canonical elements is shown in Table 8.1. As correspondences and points of emphasis vary among traditions, feel free to modify them to your liking or substitute your own.

Regarding the practical functions of the elements, earth provides structure, water provides cohesion, fire facilitates formation and maturation, air permits movement and change, and space reveals boundaries (see *Maha-hatthipadopama Sutta* (MN 28; Bhikkhu (Trans.), 2003)). The fifth element of space can be interpreted differently from its Hindu counterpart [San. *ākāśa*; clear sky or space], as space (sometimes translated as "void") emphasizes the Buddhist concept of *śūnyatā* [San. void or emptiness].

Table 8.1. *Tibetan Buddhist Elemental Correspondences*

Attribute	Earth	Water	Fire	Air[a]	Space
Direction	South	East	West	North	Center
Color	Yellow	Blue	Red	Green	White
Aggregate [San.]	*Vedanā* [sensation]	*Rūpa* [form]	*Saṃjñā* [conception]	*Saṃskāra* [emotion]	*Vijñāna* [cognition]
Buddha [San.][b]	*Ratna-sambhava*	*Akṣobhya*	*Amitābha*	*Amoghasiddhi*	*Vairocana*
Poison	Pride	Hate	Lust	Envy	Delusion
Wisdom	Equalizing	Mirror	Discriminating	All-Accomplishing	Reality Perfection
Seed syllable	*TRAṂ*	*HŪṂ*	*HRĪḤ*	*ĀḤ*	*OṂ*
Mudrā [San.]	*Varada* [giving]	*Bhūsparśa* [earth-touching]	*Samādhi* [meditation]	*Abhaya* [fearlessness]	*Dharma-cakra* [wheel-turning]
Implement	Jewel	*Vajra*	Lotus	*Viśvavajra* (double *vajra*)	Eight-spoked wheel

Information is adapted from Beer (2003), Bhattacharyya (1980), and Thurman (Trans.) (1994). Romanized Sanskrit is in italics. [a]"Air" is sometimes called "wind" to emphasize its mobile nature. [b]In some traditions the Buddhas of water (*Akṣobhya*) and space (*Vairocana*) are switched.

A sixth element (consciousness) is sometimes mentioned in Buddhist literature (see *Dhatu-vibhanga Sutta* (MN 140; Bhikkhu (Trans.), 1997)). It is discussed extensively in esoteric Buddhism. The Shingon tradition of Japan (Shingon Buddhist International Institute, 1998/1999) elaborates:

The great element that is the earth refers to how the Earth is the Mother of life on earth. The great element of water is the water of life that gives moisture to all things and nurtures the power of life. The great element of fire is the energy that is possessed by fire and is the working of life that gives heat and vitality to living things. The great element of wind is best thought of as the breath of the entire universe, it is constant movement. Each breath we

*take is life itself. The great element of space is the vast
and eternal life of the universe that envelops all things.
The great element of consciousness is the life of the spirit
that is in all things and is the functioning of wisdom.*
(par. 7)

Mantras and Mudrās

Elemental *mantras* have the ability to enlighten us physically,
mentally, and spiritually through purification of the
aggregates. To recite a *mantra*, sit in a comfortable position
and clear your mind. Feel free to incorporate an appropriate
mudrā or *asana*. Repetitions are typically counted on a string
of prayer beads. A basic elemental *mantra* from the Tibetan
tradition is *OM* _____ *HŪM*, with the blank holding an
elemental Buddha's name. This formula serves to purify and
unite your consciousness with an elemental Buddha. The
Sanskrit word *OM* symbolizes "...the pure, exalted body,
speech and mind of a Buddha and Bodhisattva" (Rinpoche,
n.d., par. 2). It is the sound of the universe. The Sanskrit word
HŪM symbolizes "the union of method and wisdom leads to
pure exalted body, speech and mind of enlightened beings"
(Rinpoche, n.d., par. 5). More information on *mantras*
(including a pronunciation guide), should you choose to
pursue it, is available at *Visible Mantra* (http://www.visible
mantra.org/).

Various *mudrās* may also be incorporated into Buddhist
practice. These specialized gestures connect us with
particular concepts and energies. Here, we will be using
them to more deeply connect with the Buddhist elements.
Mudrās frequently involve use of the hands and fingers,
though some may involve the entire body. The *mudrā*
associated with each elemental Buddha is shown in Figure
8.2. More information on *mudrās* (including an illustration
guide), should you choose to pursue it, is available at *Light
of Asia* (http://www.buddhas-online.com/mudras.html).

Ratnasaṃbhava   *Akṣobhya*   *Amitābha*   *Amoghasiddhi*   *Vairocana*

Figure 8.2. Elemental Buddha *mudrās*. Each elemental Buddha is associated with a particular *mudrā* (Bhattacharyya, 1980). From left to right, they are: earth, *Ratnasaṃbhava, varada* [San. giving]; water, *Akṣobhya, bhūsparśa* [earth-touching]; fire, *Amitābha, samādhi* [meditation]; air, *Amoghasiddhi, abhaya* [fearlessness]; and space, *Vairocana, dharmacakra* [wheel-turning].

Buddhist Architecture: The *Stūpa*

The elements contribute to Buddhist architecture. This is evident in the *stūpa* [San. heap], a structure designed to house Buddhist relics (Kumar, 2003; Trainor, 2006). The earliest discovered *stūpas* are simple in design and built from perishable material, whereas later ones were typically built with a durable stone (Kumar, 2003). They may share a distant link with Vedic funeral practices (Trainor, 2006). They are objects of meditation and contemplation, serving as a bridge between the human realm and *nirvāṇa* (Trainor, 2006).

Each structural component of the *stūpa* corresponds to a Buddhist element (Figure 8.3). Their sequence from the ground up reflects how our bodies return to the elements upon death. Sangharakshita (1996) writes:

At death, the solid parts of the body revert to earth. The fluid parts – blood and the rest – revert to water. The vital heat in the body returns to fire, being absorbed into the total heat and warmth of the universe. The air which fills our lungs is just exhaled into the atmosphere. When our physical body ceases to exist, the space it occupies merges into the great space. (p. 78)

Figure 8.3. The *stūpa*. Tibetan Buddhist color correspondences and three-dimensional shapes, from the ground up, are: earth, yellow cube; water, blue sphere; fire, red cone; air, green semicircle or crescent; and space, white drop (Beer, 2003; Sangharakshita, 1996). This color scheme is consistent with the one presented in *The Tibetan Book of the Dead* (Thurman (Trans.), 1994). In some traditions blue and white are switched (Beer, 2003). The shapes are always present in this order, but may vary in color or size due to cultural influences and architectural styles. Complex *stūpas* are often embellished with additional decorations.

space

air

fire

water

earth

The shapes are most obvious in simpler structures like grave monuments. Though the architecture of these structures evolved as Buddhism spread, key shapes representing the elements are still present. If you look closely, you can find them in the Chinese pagoda and some Japanese architecture.

You may think of the *stūpa* as a miniature representation of the universe (Bhattacharyya, 1980). The *stūpa* is useful in ritual work and serves as an excellent focal point for meditation. It may also be dedicated as a shrine to honor your ancestors. It is possible to build your own small *stūpa* at home. All you have to do is make the shapes and stick them together. Color-coding them is optional. A simple *stūpa* can be made from construction paper or *papier-mâché*. If you are artsy, making the shapes from wood, glass, or something else is another possibility. If your *stūpa* is made of durable enough material it may be placed outside.

Buddhism in Chaos Magic

Buddhism and chaos magic are a popular combination. The two are exceedingly compatible with each other.

Various Buddhas and Bodhisattvas associated with the elements may be invoked or evoked. Divination for illumination purposes may be performed while in a meditative state. Buddhist objects or symbols may be enchanted for a variety of purposes. Prayer flags may be created and suspended in a windy place to carry their blessings out into the world. Illumination may focus on personal transformation, self-awareness, or reaching *nirvāṇa*. The aggregates associated with each element may be purified through meditation, *mantras*, *mudrās*, and more. Drawings or *maṇḍalas* may also be contemplated.

Rites applying the Buddhist elements are outlined below. Though they are chaos magic-inspired, they are consistent with the nature of each element in the Buddhist paradigm and serve to familiarize you with their underlying forces. Rites are intentionally ordered to reflect the *stūpa* sequence from the ground up.

Earth: *Stūpa* Meditation

You will need your *stūpa*. Additional meditation paraphernalia is not required, but feel free to include incense or any other items important in your tradition. Here, you will become acquainted with the elemental aggregates and explore how they manifest in your physical body. Sit cross-legged facing your *stūpa* to begin.

Procedure:
1. *Earth*: Contemplate *vedanā*. Focus your attention towards your skeleton. Spend a few moments experiencing its importance as the foundation of your body – it is solid, strong, and supportive.
2. *Water:* Contemplate *rūpa*. Focus your attention towards your bloodstream. Spend a few moments experiencing how your blood is mobile and cohesive. Both of these properties are necessary for blood to

transport substances throughout the body.

3. *Fire*: Contemplate *samjñā*. Focus your attention towards your metabolism and body temperature. Experience the heat your body emanates. Sense how this energy radiates upwards and out.

4. *Air*: Contemplate *saṃskāra*. Focus your attention towards your breathing. Observe how your internal movements accommodate inhalation and exhalation. Feel your diaphragm push up and down. Experience the dynamic nature of the overall breathing process.

5. *Space*: Contemplate *vijñāna*. Focus your attention towards the physical space your body occupies. Spend a few moments perceiving the boundary separating you from the external environment. Spend a few moments observing how the activities of the other elements lie within this boundary.

6. When you are finished, open your eyes and take a moment to become reacquainted with your surroundings. Once you are reoriented you may stand up.

7. Record your results in your magical diary.

Water: Sand *Maṇḍala* Creation

The stunning sand *maṇḍala* creations of Tibetan Buddhism bless those that see them, as well as the environment (Samten, n.d.). They are geometric images that serve as spiritual and ritual symbols. Each design is unique and conveys a specific blessing and representation of the universe. These symbolic expressions of enlightenment also serve as "an essence-protecting environment" (Thurman (Trans.), 1994, p. 265). The overall sand *maṇḍala* creation and destruction process is highly ritualized and takes many years of training to execute properly.

Here, you will design and create your own small sand *maṇḍala*. You will need scratch paper, a small piece of poster board, a pencil, a ruler, a drawing compass, scissors, plastic bags, tape, a spoon, a jar or vase, a large paintbrush, and colored sand. Traditionally, the sand is made from different colored crushed stones, but any crushable natural material may be used (Bryant, 2003). Instructions are:

1. Meditate on a blessing you want to offer the world. Let your intuition guide you. Your blessing will influence the overall design of your *maṇḍala*.

2. Meditate on the overall design of your *maṇḍala*. Choose symbolism that has personal relevance to you. Create a draft of your design on scratch paper. Use your ruler and compass if necessary. Determine which colors of sand will go where. For example, if I wanted to design a *maṇḍala* with the intent of elemental harmony, I could include well-balanced sections featuring images of the elemental Buddhas their symbols, or other elemental correspondences. Symbolism related to harmony could also be included. If you would like to use Buddhist symbols in your design, *The Handbook of Tibetan Buddhist Symbols* (Beer, 2003) is a good resource.

3. Transfer your sketch onto the poster board. The compass and ruler will ensure even circles and straight lines. While drawing, visualize the overarching goal of the *maṇḍala*. Feel free to incorporate additional prayers or chants as well.

4. Prepare your sand. To infuse each grain with a blessing, visualize the overarching goal of the *maṇḍala* as you place the different colors of sand in plastic bags.

5. Place your poster board on a table or other level surface where wind, pets, etc. cannot reach it. Begin in the center of your *maṇḍala* and work outwards, filling in sections with the appropriate sand. Lay down each section with intent. To pour the sand from the plastic bag, cut a small hole in the corner. Holes

of various sizes can be made – each will have a different impact on pouring. Gently tap or pour the sand out of the bag onto your design. Tape the corner of the bag when not in use to prevent sand from leaking out. Feel free to incorporate additional prayers or chants consistent with the *maṇḍala's* purpose while pouring the sand.

6. Enjoy your *maṇḍala*. You may take a picture if you'd like. When you gaze at the *maṇḍala*, remember its purpose and visualize its blessings radiating outwards.

7. When ready to destroy your *maṇḍala*, meditate on the impermanence of all things. Using your large paintbrush, sweep the sand from the outer portion of the *maṇḍala* towards the center in straight lines. After you have formed a pile of sand in the middle of your poster board, sweep it into your jar. To get the last few grains of sand, pick up the poster board and funnel it into the jar.

8. Bring your jar of sand to a place with naturally occurring running water. Still visualizing the *maṇḍala's* purpose, pour the sand into the water. Rinse the jar to get the last few grains out. Visualize the grains carrying your blessing into the ocean and spreading throughout the world. Additional chants or prayers can also be said during this time.

Fire: Expanding Awareness

You will need prayer beads or another counting device to keep track of *mantra* repetitions. Traditional Tibetan *mālās* [San. garlands] have 108 beads to signify the 108 *dharmas* (Beer, 2003). Additional meditation paraphernalia is not required, but feel free to include incense or any other items important in your tradition. Here, you will perform 108 repetitions of a *mantra* for each element while in the *mudrā* of its corresponding Buddha. This serves to enhance your understanding of each elemental Buddha and the aggregates they personify. Sit cross-legged facing your *stūpa* to begin. The elemental shapes may be used as focal points.

Statement of Intent:
It is my will expand my awareness of the aggregates.

Procedure:
1. *Earth*: Form *varada*. Chant **OM RATNASAMBHAVA TRAM** 108 times. When you reach the end of your beads, observe how you feel.
2. *Water*: Form *bhūsparśa*. Chant **OM AKṢOBHYA HŪM** 108 times. When you reach the end of your beads, observe how you feel.
3. *Fire*: Form *samādhi*. Chant **OM AMITĀBHA HRĪḤ** 108 times. When you reach the end of your beads, observe how you feel.
4. *Air*: Form *abhaya*. Chant **OM AMOGHASIDDHI ĀḤ** 108 times. When you reach the end of your beads, observe how you feel.
5. *Space*: Form *dharmacakra*. Chant **OM VAIROCANA OM** 108 times. When you reach the end of your beads, observe how you feel.
6. When you are finished, open your eyes and take a moment to become reacquainted with your surroundings. Once you are reoriented you may stand up.
7. Record your results in your magical diary.

Air: Prayer Flag Creation

Prayer flags date back to the ancient world and are a common sight around Buddhist temples. Flags blowing into the wind are believed to bring life, good fortune, health, and wealth to all sentient beings. They are not haphazardly designed; much ritual and care go into their creation. The five colors repeat in the blue, white, red, yellow, and green pattern and bear elemental significance. Prayer flags may be vertical or horizontal and should be hung in a high place so the wind may carry their petitions into the surrounding area. As the wind blows the threads disperse, reminding us of the impermanence of even the best intentions.

Here, you will design and create your own prayer flag. You will need markers, scratch paper, equally sized squares of cloth (in blue, white, red, yellow, and green), a long piece of string, scissors, glue, and any other embellishments you want to decorate your flags with. Instructions are:

1. Meditate on what blessings you want to offer the world. Let your intuition guide you. Popular choices include world peace, ending hunger, and eradicating disease.

2. Each cloth square will hold one prayer. For each prayer, meditate on the overall design to be placed on a cloth square. Choose symbolism that has personal relevance to you. Create a draft of your design on scratch paper. For example, if I wanted to design a square with the intent of world peace, I could include peace signs, doves, olive branches, and other symbols of peace from various cultures. The word "peace" written in different languages could also be included. If you would like to use Buddhist symbols in your design, *The Handbook of Tibetan Buddhist Symbols* (Beer, 2003) is a good resource.

3. After you are satisfied with your designs, transfer them to the cloth squares. Create each square with intent while visualizing its outcome. Use whatever fabric color you want. Repeating prayers is okay, as is using different designs on different squares for the

same prayer. Leave the top 2-3cm of each square undecorated.

4. After the squares have dried, arrange them so they repeat in the blue, white, red, yellow, and green sequence. After they are ordered to your liking, turn them face down to prepare for gluing.

5. Lay the string horizontally across the top of your first square, 1cm below the top. Leave excess string at the end of your flag, so it may be hung later. Squeeze glue across the back of the cloth, slightly below the string. Fold the top part of the cloth over onto the glue, so that the string is contained in a pocket. Press down. A heavy object may also be placed on top so it may securely dry.

6. Repeat the gluing process for the other squares. Leave minimal space between the sequence of squares, so they are positioned as closely together as possible along the string. After gluing the last square, leave excess string at the end of your flag so it may be hung later. Cut the string if necessary. Leave your flags to dry. The finished product should resemble Figure 8.4.

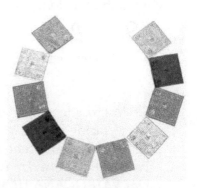

Figure 8.4. Tibetan prayer flag. Individual squares are connected via a long string, with excess left at each end to facilitate hanging. They traditionally follow a repeating color sequence of blue, white, red, green, and yellow.

You're done! Decide when and where you will hang up your final product. Prayer flags should be placed in a locale where the wind can blow on them. Alternatively, you can give them to someone as a gift. It is a good omen to receive prayer flags as a present. Whatever you do, don't lay them on the ground or put them in the trash – they are sacred objects! The traditional way to dispose of old prayer flags is to burn them. The smoke will carry the messages up to the heavens. To learn more about Tibetan prayer flags, *New World Encyclopedia* (http://www.newworldencyclopedia.org/entry/Prayer_flag) is a starting point.

Space: *Vairocana* Invocation

Vairocana is the "Illuminator" associated with water or space (Beer, 2003, p. 235). His name is sometimes transliterated as *Vairochana* because it is more phonetically accurate (Thurman (Trans.), 1994). As the Buddha of space, he sits in the center surrounded by the other elemental Buddhas. He is mentioned in the *Brahma Net Sutra*, *Flower Garland Sutra*, and more. He is also a major figure in the Shingon tradition. Statues of *Vairocana* are typically large, reminding us that emptiness is abundant and all things are impermanent. Here, we will invoke *Vairocana* to gain insight into his wisdom.

Statement of Intent:
It is my will to invoke *Vairocana*.

Procedure:
1. Sit in cross-legged in the center of your working space, facing your *stūpa*. Close your eyes, take a few deep breaths, and center yourself.
2. Form the *dharmacakra* [wheel-turning] *mudrā*. Chant *OM VAIROCANA HŪM* 108 times.
3. Still in this position, chant *OM* 108 times. With each repetition, visualize yourself glowing brighter and brighter in a brilliant white.

4. While radiating this light, visualize yourself sitting atop a golden, eight-spoke wheel. Recite the words of *Vairocana*, as given in the *Brahma Net Sutra* (trans. 2000):

    Now I, Vairocana Buddha,
    Am sitting atop a lotus pedestal;
    On a thousand flowers surrounding me
    Are a thousand Sakyamuni Buddhas.
    Each flower supports a hundred million worlds;
    In each world a Sakyamuni Buddha appears.
    All are seated beneath a Bodhi-tree,
    All simultaneously attain Buddhahood. (par. 18)

5. Observe how you feel.
6. When you are finished, open your eyes and take a moment to become reacquainted with your surroundings. Once you are reoriented you may stand up.
7. Record your results in your magical diary.
8. After you are finished you may also read from the *Brahma Net Sutra*. It describes the moral code of the Bodhisattva and is available at *Young Men's Buddhist Association of America* (http://www.ymba.org/books/brahma-net-sutra-moral-code-bodhisattva).

Chapter 8 Homework

After taking notes on the chapter, magical practice should be commenced for a minimum of 30 minutes each day for the remainder of the month. Perform the assignments in the order presented. Remember to document your efforts in your magical diary.

1. Meditate on the Buddhist elements and their aggregates for a minimum of 10 minutes each day. How do they affect your life? How do you interact with them?

2. Identify the poisons and wisdoms you harbor in the context of Buddhist cosmology. Which destination are you headed towards in your next life? What steps can you take to land in a more desirable realm, or escape the death-rebirth cycle entirely?

3. Meditate on the elemental associations for each Buddha. Then, "think in fives" to discover their underlying rationale. You may also rearrange any traditional associations to suit your personal practice if necessary.

4. Investigate the effects of the elemental *mantras* and *mudrās*. To begin, separately practice each one to determine its individual effects on your consciousness. Then, perform the *mantra* and *mudrā* for an element together. Document your results and any insights in your magical diary.

5. Create a small *stūpa* for meditation and magical practice. It can be as simple or as elaborate as you'd like. Then, meditate on the arrangement of each element in the overall structure. How does each shape interact with its neighbors? What would happen to the overall structure if the shapes were placed in a different sequence?

6. Perform the chaos magic-inspired rites to experience the Buddhist elements. Rites are intentionally ordered to reflect the sequence of elements in the *stūpa* from the ground up.

Chapter 9
Chinese *Wǔxíng* [Five Phases]

The history of the Chinese "elements" cannot be traced as closely as the western elements, but it is clear they were well established by the time of the *Hàn* Dynasty (202 BCE – 220 CE) before the import of Buddhism into China (Demerath, 2003). Both Daoism and Confucian thought became popular during this time, and classics like the *Dàodéjīng* [Chi. *Book of the Way and Virtue*] and *Shūjīng* [*Book of Documents*] indicate the Chinese were already "thinking in fives." *Zōu Yǎn* provides the earliest known account of the *wǔxíng* in the 3rd Century BCE. Though the original texts are lost, they are discussed in the *Shǐjì* [*Records of the Grand Historian*] of *Hàn* Dynasty historian *Sīmǎ Qiān*.

The *wǔxíng* are not physical elements. They are "phases" or "agents" that represent five different movements or tendencies of energy (see Chen, 1996; Selin, 1997). They have been used to describe cycles of natural phenomena, government successions, bodily organ interactions, medicinal properties of plants, and more. Chinese characters for the five phases are shown in Figure 9.1.

木	火	土	金	水
wood	fire	earth	metal	water

Figure 9.1. Chinese phase characters. To make a colored image for your notes, traditional color correspondences are: wood [Chi. *mù*], blue/green; fire [*huǒ*], red; earth [*tǔ*], yellow; metal [*jīn*], white; and water [*shuǐ*], black (Wang, 2000). The character describing wood (青; *qīng*) means blue or green (Bates, 2007), but is often interpreted as green (Wang, 120; Wen, 2016).

139

Soror Velchanes

Daoist Model of Cosmology

Daoism has roots in Chinese shamanism and predates the *Hàn* Dynasty (Demerath, 2003). Perhaps some of these shamans are the "ancient masters" mentioned in the *Dàodéjīng* (Tzu, trans. 1989, Ch. 15). In this model, the five phases emerge as a natural result of the *Dào* (Ch. 42; Figure 9.2).

In the beginning was the *Dào*, an undifferentiated unity beyond comprehension (Tzu, trans. 1989, Ch. 32). A state of duality (*yīn* and *yáng*) emerges from the *Dào*. *Yīn* energy is dark, receptive, and contractive, whereas *yáng* energy is light, active, and expansive (Perkins, 1999/2013; Wen, 2016). The constant flux of these opposites fuels the flow of *qì*. The *tàijítú* symbol (Figure 9.2b) emphasizes the cyclical nature of their interactions. The peak of an energy contains its decline, as the seed of the opposite energy resides within it. The five phases emerge from the interactions of *yīn* and *yang*, and are also cyclical in nature. The *bāguà* [Chi. eight symbols] and 64 *Yìjīng* [*Book of Changes*] hexagrams also manifest from the *Dào*. Altogether, interactions among these energies produce the "ten thousand things" of the phenomenal world (Tzu, trans. 1989, Ch. 42).

Figure 9.2. Daoist model of cosmology.
The undifferentiated (a) *Dào* produces (b) *yīn* [Chi. shady side] and *yáng* [sunny side] energies. Their interactions produce the *wǔxíng* [five phases], (c) eight *bāguà* trigrams (*yīn* is represented by the broken line, and *yáng* by the solid line), (d) 64 *Yìjīng* hexagrams, and (e) the "ten thousand things" comprising the phenomenal world (Tzu, trans. 1989, Ch. 42).

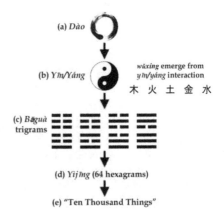

(a) *Dào*

(b) *Yīn/Yáng*

wǔxíng emerge from *yīn/yáng* interaction
木 火 土 金 水

(c) *Bāguà* trigrams

(d) *Yìjīng* (64 hexagrams)

(e) "Ten Thousand Things"

Ancient practitioners strived to live in harmony with the *Dào*. The Daoist model of cosmology evolved and perpetuated for over two millennia, inspiring Chinese spirituality, philosophy, government, medicine, and more. More information on Daoism, should you choose to pursue it, is available at *Center of Traditional Taoist Studies* (http://www.tao.org/), *Personal Tao* (http://personaltao. com/teachings/taoism/taoism-101/), and *Taoism.net* (http://taoism.net/tao/).

Confucian Philosophy

Confucius [Chi. *Kǒngzǐ*] was born in northeastern China around 551 BCE (Chin, 2007). He was a "common gentleman" who moved into the arena of state government (Chin, 2007, p. 13). In his 50s he resigned and travelled from state to state, ultimately becoming a teacher in his 60s a few years before he died (Chin, 2007; Eno (Trans.), 2015). Confucius examined society, nobleness, and virtue during a period of ideological crisis when feudal lords were losing power (Chin, 2007; Eno (Trans.), 2015). He relied on his knowledge of history and awareness of cultural practices to try and shift the dominant social and political paradigms of the day (Chin, 2007). Though concrete facts about his life are sparse (Chin, 2007), his teachings are recorded in *Lúnyǔ* [*The Analects*]. Some fundamental Confucian concepts relevant to our elemental work are:

仁 [rén]:
Confucius describes *rén* [Chi. goodness, humanity] as "knowing others" (Eno (Trans.), 2015, 12.22). A person of humanity is "…someone who is thoroughly relational in their thoughts, feelings, and actions" (trans. 2015, p. 119). This virtue allows leaders to effectively govern (trans. 2015, 12.19).

禮 [lǐ]:

Dedication to *lǐ* [Chi. ritual] is a cornerstone of the Confucian school (Eno (Trans.), 2015, p. 118). Interactions of virtuous people are governed by following proper protocols, and to Confucian followers, it is the essence of civilization itself. Filial piety (honoring your biological ancestors) is among the tenets (trans. 2015, 2.5).

義 [yì]:

Moral disposition and ability to successfully perform good deeds are important aspects of this characteristic. *Yì* [Chi. righteousness, appropriateness] encompasses loyalty, reciprocity, and more (Eno, (Trans.), 2015, 4.15). A key Confucian rule of reciprocity is, "That which you do not desire, do not do to others" (trans. 2015, 15.24).

***

Numerous efforts were made to integrate *wǔxíng* into Confucian thought (e.g., *Chūnqiū Fánlù* [*Luxuriant Dew of the Spring and Autumn Annals*]; *Tài Xuán Jīng* [*Canon of Supreme Mystery*]; *Báihǔ Tōng* [*Comprehensive Discussions in White Tiger Hall*]...), though not all Confucian thinkers accepted *wǔxíng* cosmology (see *Lùnhéng*, [*Critical Essays*]). Confucian thinking allows us to discover truth in ourselves and improve everything around us. This philosophy spread from ancient China and is present in many parts of the world today where it still holds relevance.

Chinese Magic

Many Chinese magical practices have roots in shamanism and were present well before the *Hàn* Dynasty (Marshall, 2006). Though esoteric practices are by no means unified, many concern themselves with maintaining harmony between the heavenly and earthly realms (Marshall, 2006; Wen, 2016). Some key components of Chinese practice relevant to our elemental work are:

Spirit Money:
The practice of burning paper offerings dates back to at least the reign of *Hé Dì* (89 CE – 106 CE) during the late *Hàn* Dynasty (Scott, 2007). Burning allows the offerings to transcend the physical world and reach gods, ghosts, and ancestors (Scott, 2007). Papers are burned for a variety of purposes, including giving thanks, requesting assistance, or helping the deceased in the afterlife (Blake, 2011; Scott, 2007). Regarding the latter, Hell money is the most common form of spirit money seen in the west. It is frequently offered at funerals and certain festivals. The story goes that missionaries told the Chinese they were "going to Hell," so they thought "Hell" was their term for the afterlife. Hell money may be purchased in many Asian supermarkets or online.

Firecrackers:
Firecrackers originated in China, and records indicate they were used as early as the *Táng* Dynasty (607 CE – 907 CE) (Wong et al. (Trans.), 2012). Ritually, firecrackers are used to purify an area by ridding it of hostile spirits (Blake, 2011; Feng & Du, 2015). In rites to the dead they conclude the service by driving them away. Spirits lingering around the living may pose unnecessary danger (Blake, 2011). Many aspects of funerary rites also bear elemental significance.

Ancestor Veneration:
The practice of honoring biological ancestors has roots in Chinese shamanism and was around well before the popularization of Daoist or Confucian thought (Kern, 2009). Filial piety is a recurring theme in many traditions, thus it follows that honoring the deceased remains a large part of esoteric practice. The simplest way to honor the ancestors is to offer them food and drink (Eno (Trans.), 2015). In Daoism, and many folk religions, incense may be offered along with prayers and paper offerings (Wen,

2016). In *The Analects*, Confucius encourages the living to be respectful towards ghosts, but to otherwise keep them at a distance (Eno (Trans.), 2015, 6.22). He also remarks that it is one's duty to honor their ancestors (trans. 2015, 2.24).

The *Wŭxíng* [Five Phases] Model

The correlative power of the *wŭxíng* permitted successful integration with other systems, leading to its eventual dominance in early China (Wang, 2000). The fundamental processes each phase represents are viewed as the expression of heavenly cycles or patterns. The phases are dynamic and interact with each other in distinct ways. One phase is not superior to another, and there is no "best" phase. The *Shūjīng* describes the five phases in *Hóng Fàn* (quoted in Chen, 1996):

Wu-xing: *1. water, 2. fire, 3. wood, 4. metal, 5. earth.*

Water [is of the quality] that is soaking and descending.

Fire [is of the quality] that is blazing and rising.

Wood [is of the quality] that allows curving and aligning.

Metal [is of the quality] that allows moulding and solidifying.

Earth [is of the quality] that allows farming and harvest. (p. 200)

A plethora of *wŭxíng* correspondences exist. Each phase is associated with a specific color, direction, season, quarter guardian, animal type, and more, as shown in Table 9.1. As correspondences and points of emphasis vary among traditions, feel free to modify them to your liking or substitute your own.

Table 9.1. Wǔxíng *Correspondences*

Attribute	Wood	Fire	Earth	Metal	Water
Color	Blue/ Green[a]	Red	Yellow	White	Black
Direction	East	South	Center	West	North
Season	Spring	Summer	Mid-summer[b]	Autumn	Winter
Quarter guardian	Azure Dragon	Vermillion Bird	N/A[c]	White Tiger	Black Tortoise
Animal type	Scaly	Feathered	Naked[d]	Hairy	Shelled
Sense	Sight	Speech	Taste	Smell	Hearing
Human finger	Index	Middle	Thumb	Ring	Little
Weather	Windy	Hot	Humid	Dry	Cold
Work	Birth, sprouting	Growth, blooming	Flourishing	Punishing, severity	Death, closing up
Yīn/Yáng state	Lesser *yáng*	Greater *yáng*	Balance	Lesser *yīn*	Greater *yīn*

Information is adapted from Wang (2000) and Wen (2016). [a]I have seen some practitioners assign green to wood and blue to water. Perhaps this is due to Buddhist influence. [b]I have seen some practitioners attribute the change of seasons, or all four seasons, to earth. [c]Sometimes humans are placed in the center, surrounded by the four guardians. [d]Humans are "naked" animals.

The phases may be arranged to reflect different cycles of progression. The two most commonly encountered sequences are the *xiāngshēng* [Chi. mutual generation] and *xiāngkè* [mutual conquest] cycles (Wang, 2000; Figure 9.3). In the *xiāngshēng* cycle, one phase (the "parent") nourishes, strengthens, or promotes development of another (the "child"). The phases in Table 9.1 are ordered in this sequence. In the *xiāngkè* cycle, one phase (the "grandparent") controls, weakens, or restrains another (the "grandchild"). These interactions are akin to the ones in the game rock-scissors-paper, but with five components instead of three.

Soror Velchanes

Figure 9.3. Xiāngshēng [mutual generation] and *xiāngkè* [mutual conquest] cycles. The mutual generation cycle (solid lines) is as follows – wood (as fuel) produces fire; fire burns to produce earth (ash); earth produces metal (from mining); metal (on its surface) produces water (as dew); and water produces wood (by feeding plants). The "parent" nourishes the "child." The  mutual conquest cycle (dashed lines) is as follows – wood (as a plow) conquers earth; earth (as a dam) conquers water; water conquers fire (by extinguishing it); fire conquers metal (by melting it); and metal (as an axe) conquers wood (by chopping it). The "grandparent" controls the "grandchild."

The Phases and Health

There appears to be no mention of *wǔxíng* in a medical context before the *Qín* Dynasty (221 BCE – 207 BCE) (Yuqun, 2011). The first recorded mention in ancient medical texts is in the *Huángdì Nèijīng* [Chi. *Inner Canon of the Yellow Emperor*], finalized in the 1st Century BCE. The first part of the work is the *Sù Wèn* [*Basic Questions*], which discusses the theoretical basis for Chinese medicine and diagnostic methods. The second part of the work is the *Língshūjīng* [*Spiritual Pivot*], which discusses acupuncture in great detail.

In traditional Chinese medicine, *yīn*/*yáng* and *wǔxíng* explain bodily activities and disease (Maciocia, 2015; Yuqun, 2011). Our *qì* circulates through meridians (channels) that lead to different organs. The balance of this *qì* is responsible for our good health or lack thereof (Maciocia, 2015; Yuqun, 2011). In this model, disease originates from four major sources:

1. Excess "child" taking too much from its "parent"
2. Deficiency of a "child" due to undernourishment from its "parent"
3. Excess "grandparent" conquering its "grandchild"

4. Deficiency of a "grandparent" due to rebellion from its "grandchild"

Diagnosis is primarily based on correlating patient signs and symptoms with *wŭxíng* correspondences (Yuqun, 2011; Table 9.2). The five phases correspond to two organs each – one is associated with *yīn* energy, and the other is associated with *yáng* energy (Maciocia, 2015). The *xiāngshēng* and *xiāngkè* relationships carry over to dictate relationships and interactions among organs.

Table 9.2. *Traditional Chinese Medicine* Wŭxíng *Correspondences*

Attribute	Wood	Fire	Earth	Metal	Water
Yīn organ	Liver	Heart[a]	Spleen	Lungs	Kidneys
Yáng organ	Gall bladder	Small intestine[b]	Stomach	Large intestine	Bladder
Sense organ	Eyes	Tongue	Mouth	Nose	Ears
Tissue	Sinews[c]	Vessels	Muscles	Skin	Bones
Taste	Sour	Bitter	Sweet	Acrid/ Pungent	Salty
Smell	Rancid	Scorched	Fragrant	Rotten	Putrid
Sound	Shouting	Laughing	Singing	Lamenting	Groaning

Information is adapted from Maciocia (2015). [a]The pericardium is another *yīn* organ associated with fire. [b]The "Triple Burner" is another *yáng* organ associated with fire. It is an invisible organ spread across the chest and abdominal region, and regulates *qì* and water flow. [c]Sinews are tendons and ligaments.

Treatment under the traditional Chinese model focuses on correcting the source of disharmony and restoring balance (Maciocia, 2015). Physicians may prescribe various diet and exercise regimens, herbal medicines, moxibustion (burning substances over acupressure points), acupuncture, and more. For example, a disease caused by excess fire may be overcome by taking medicines associated with water. Likewise, since wood energy saturates the liver and gall bladder, consuming sour foods will fortify these organs.

Traditional Chinese medicine spread from ancient China and dominated eastern medical thinking, evolving over thousands of years. Though its efficacy is questionable (Barrett, 2011; National Center for Complementary and Integrative Health, 2017; Novella, 2012), it is still present in alternative medical traditions and many forms of folk medicine today.

The Phases and Psychology

Health and personality are not decoupled in traditional Chinese medicine (Maciocia, 2015; Yuqun, 2011). Each individual is composed of a unique elemental constitution, which in turn influences the personality (Maciocia, 2015). Excessive emotions may also cause disease (Xuan, 2011). Some hallmark personality traits associated with each phase follow. Information is adapted from *The Foundations of Chinese Medicine: A Comprehensive Text* (Maciocia, 2015) and "The Five Taoist Elements" (Levitt, 1998).

Wood:
The archetypal wood personality is intelligent, honest, hardworking, competitive, and a good decision maker. However, they can also be tense, overly critical, and worry excessively. The emotion associated with the wood phase is anger.

Fire:
The archetypal fire personality is warm, passionate, loving, dynamic, and an excellent observer. However, they can also be short-tempered and overanalyze situations. The emotion associated with the fire phase is happiness.

Earth:
The archetypal earth personality is steady, practical, industrious, kind, and prudent. However, they can also lack ambition and over-indulge. The emotion associated with the earth phase is sympathy.

Metal:
The archetypal metal personality is independent, focused, intense, righteous, and a leader. However, they can also be insecure and lack confidence. The emotion associated with the metal phase is grief.

Water:
The archetypal water personality is sociable, sympathetic, sensitive, reflective, and persuasive. However, they can also be indecisive or timid. The emotion associated with the water phase is fear.

Wǔxíng In Chaos Magic

I have not often seen *wǔxíng* applied to chaos magic practice, despite its usefulness. Various egregores, godforms, or pop culture characters associated with one or more phases may be invoked or evoked. Divination may be performed by casting a *yìjīng* reading. Chinese *fú* (talismans), auspicious items, or other objects may be enchanted for a variety of purposes. Spirit money or firecrackers may be ignited to appease or repel ghosts. Illumination may focus on cultivating virtue, self-awareness, or leading a balanced life.

Rites applying the Chinese phases are found below. Though they are chaos magic-inspired, they are consistent with the nature of each phase in ancient Chinese thinking and serve to familiarize you with the unique modality of each energy. Rites are intentionally ordered to reflect the sequence of phases in the *xiāngshēng* cycle.

Wood: Evocation of the Azure Dragon

The Azure Dragon is one of the four ancient Chinese constellations and quarter guardian of the east (Bates, 2007). In ancient China, it appeared in the eastern sky during the spring season (Bates, 2007). The constellation is composed of seven collections of stars corresponding to clusters in the Greco-Roman Virgo, Libra, Scorpio, and Sagittarius (Selin, 1997). It also spans seven mansions (positions) of the moon in Chinese astrology (Selin, 1997). The east corresponds to the wood phase, which represents curving, aligning, or birthing energies. Wood is also associated with our sense of charity and goodwill (Wen, 2016).

Here, we will evoke the Azure Dragon to cultivate *rén*. In China, dragons represent spiritual power, strength, and good luck (Bates, 2007). They also have the ability to control the weather, especially rain (Bates, 2007). The Azure Dragon has the power to control events (Wen, 2016).

Materials:
No materials are required. Placing incense you associate with wood and a small picture of the Azure Dragon in the east are optional.

Statement of Intent:
It is my will to cultivate *rén*.

Procedure:
1. Face east. Light your incense and place your Azure Dragon image in the east, if you have them.
2. Take a deep breath and center yourself. Visualize the *qì* flowing in your body, healthy and unhindered.
3. Face your open palms toward the east, as if you are signaling for the Azure Dragon to come down from

the sky. Continue visualizing the unobstructed flow of *qì* in your body.

4. Say:

Azure Dragon, commander of wood in the east,
I evoke you!
Guard me in my endeavors to grow
compassion, wisdom, charity, and goodwill!
Horn, neck, root, room, heart, tail, winnowing
basket,
descend from the eastern heavens!
Bless me with spiritual power, good luck,
and adaptability,
so I may cultivate *rén*!

5. Repeat the evocation until you feel the presence of the Azure Dragon. Observe how his energy impacts the *qì* in your body.
6. If you have an image of the Azure Dragon, use any preferred method of visual gnosis to charge it with your intent to cultivate personal *rén*.
7. You may also ask the Azure Dragon to share any insights he has with you. After you are finished communicating with him, thank him and send him on his way.

Banishing:
Banish with laughter. Relight your incense any time you feel it is necessary. Carry your image of the Azure Dragon to enhance personal *rén* and increase vigilance.

Fire: Lucky Red Paper Lanterns

Chinese paper lanterns are a common sight at festivals and other celebratory occasions, such as birthdays or weddings. The practice of hanging paper lanterns was popularized during the *Hàn* Dynasty (Wong et al. (Trans.),

2012). Hanging a lantern at the front door of a business or home attracts good luck (Wong et al. (Trans.), 2012). Lanterns are available in many varieties, though ones available in the west are typically made from bamboo, metal, or wooden frames and covered with thin paper. They come in a variety of shapes and colors and may be simple or elaborate in design. Fancier lanterns may be made with silk, depict auspicious symbols, illustrate historical events, or be embellished with jade stones, pearls, or tassels (Perkins, 1999/2013).

Here, we will enchant a red lantern to increase our good luck. Red is an auspicious color and symbolizes happiness, virtue, and good luck (Perkins, 1999/2013). It is also useful for attracting prosperity and warding off evil (Wen, 2016). We will first call the quarter guardians to raise energy (akin to western witches calling the quarters), and then we will construct and consecrate the lantern.

Materials:
You will need a plain red paper lantern, gold paint pens, and anything else you'd like to decorate your lantern with. Red tassels, gold colored beads, and stencils depicting auspicious good luck symbols are popular options. You may consecrate your crafting supplies beforehand if you feel it is necessary or if it is important in your tradition. A small firecracker is also optional.

Preparation:
Decide beforehand how you will decorate your lantern. Feel free to sketch your design on a piece of scratch paper. Place the lantern and crafting supplies in the center of your working area.

Statement of Intent:
It is my will to increase my good luck.

Procedure:
1. Face south. Take a deep breath and center yourself. Extend your open palms towards the sky and say, *"Vermillion Bird, commander of fire in the south, I call you!"*
2. Walk west in a quarter circle until you arrive in the west. Face west with your open palms extended towards the sky and say, *"White Tiger, commander of metal in the west, I call you!"*
3. Walk north in a quarter circle until you arrive in the north. Face north with your open palms extended towards the sky and say, *"Black Tortoise, commander of water in the north, I call you!"*
4. Walk east in a quarter circle until you arrive in the east. Face east with your open palms extended towards the sky and say, *"Azure Dragon, commander of wood in the east, I call you!"*
5. Walk south in a quarter circle until you arrive back where you began. Your circle is now complete.
6. Move into the center of your circle and face south. Say:

**Guardians of the quarters,
lend me your power!
I evoke your synergy
to increase my good luck!
May this paper lantern
serve as a conduit for
its blazing, rising growth!**

7. Chant *hǎoyùn* [Chi. good luck] to the rhythm of your heartbeat while decorating your lantern. Feel free to modify the design if your intuition deems it necessary. Visualize your good luck increasing during this creation process. Picture yourself in lucky situations or in a flow state.

8. After you are satisfied with your decorated lantern, hold it up to the southern quarter. Visualize *qì* from the quarter guardians and your personal *qì* flowing into the lantern, purifying and empowering it. Say:

**Guardians of the quarters,
lend me your power!
Consecrate this paper lantern
so it may blaze with good luck!
May it bring peace, prosperity, and harmony!
May all go well!**

9. Continue visualizing *qì* from the quarter guardians and your personal *qì* flowing into the lantern, purifying and empowering it, for as long as necessary.
10. Thank and dismiss each quarter guardian by walking to each quarter, facing it, and saying, *"[Quarter guardian], commander of [phase] in the [direction], I thank you. You are dismissed!"* Perform this in the reverse sequence you used to initially call the quarter guardians.

Banishing:
Light a small firecracker (away from people, pets, etc.) to end the rite. The firecracker will banish any spirits in the area. If you are in a place where firecrackers are not practical or are altogether prohibited, loudly clap your hands and banish with laughter instead. Hang up your lantern wherever you see fit.

Earth: Balancing *Yīn/Yáng* Energies

The earth phase personifies the balance of *yīn* and *yáng*, and is associated with harmonizing, flourishing energies. It is located centrally, surrounded by the quarter guardians. Here, we will balance our inner phases to promote health, harmony, and spiritual enlightenment.

We will first call the quarter guardians to raise energy, and then we will stand in the center and balance our energies.

Statement of Intent:
It is my will to achieve a state of perfect elemental harmony.

Procedure:
1. Face south. Take a deep breath and center yourself. Extend your open palms towards the sky and say, *"Vermillion Bird, commander of fire in the south, I call you!"*
2. Walk west in a quarter circle until you arrive in the west. Face west with your open palms extended towards the sky and say, *"White Tiger, commander of metal in the west, I call you!"*
3. Walk north in a quarter circle until you arrive in the north. Face north with your open palms extended towards the sky and say, *"Black Tortoise, commander of water in the north, I call you!"*
4. Walk east in a quarter circle until you arrive in the east. Face east with your open palms extended towards the sky and say, *"Azure Dragon, commander of wood in the east, I call you!"*
5. Walk south in a quarter circle until you arrive back where you began. Your circle is now complete.
6. Move into the center of your circle and face south. Visualize the *qì* flowing in your body, healthy and unhindered. Feel the phases within and around you.
7. Outstretch your arms and say:

   Guardians of the quarters,
   lend me your power!
   I evoke your synergy
   to balance *yīn* and *yáng*,
   heaven and earth,
   earth and man,
   man and heaven!

8. Continue visualizing the unobstructed flow of *qì* in your body. Chant *pínghéng* [Chi. balance] until you feel balanced and refreshed. You may optionally anchor this state of "elemental harmony" to a word, gesture, or something else so you may recall this state in the future.

Banishing:
Banish with laughter if you feel it is necessary.

Metal: Evocation of the White Tiger

The White Tiger is one of the four ancient Chinese constellations and quarter guardian of the west (Selin, 1997; Wen, 2016). In ancient China, it was prominent in the autumn sky (Perkins, 1999/2013). The constellation is composed of seven collections of stars corresponding to clusters in the Greco-Roman Andromeda, Aries, Taurus, and Orion (Selin, 1997). It also spans seven mansions (positions) of the moon in Chinese astrology (Selin, 1997). The west corresponds to the metal phase, which represents molding, solidifying, or contracting energies. Metal is also associated with our instinct, perception, and ambition (Wen, 2016).

Here, we will evoke the White Tiger to cultivate *yì*. In China, tigers represent earthly power. They are allies of good and enemies of evil (Perkins, 1999/2013). They protect human life, and keep away diseases, evil spirits, and other disasters (Perkins, 1999/2013). The White Tiger has the power of clairvoyance (Wen, 2016).

Materials:
No materials are required. Placing incense you associate with metal and a small picture of the White Tiger in the west are optional.

Statement of Intent:
It is my will to cultivate *yì*.

Procedure:

1. Face west. Light your incense and place your White Tiger image in the west, if you have them.
2. Take a deep breath and center yourself. Visualize the *qì* flowing in your body, healthy and unhindered.
3. Face your open palms toward the west, as if you are signaling for the White Tiger to come down from the sky. Continue visualizing the unobstructed flow of *qì* in your body.
4. Say:

   White Tiger, commander of metal in the west,
   I evoke you!
   Guard me in my endeavors of righteousness,
   upholding good and vanquishing evil!
   Legs, bond, stomach, mane, net,
   turtle beak, three stars,
   descend from the western heavens!
   Bless me with personal power, perception,
   and ambition,
   so I may cultivate *yì*!

5. Repeat the evocation until you feel the presence of the White Tiger. Observe how his energy impacts the *qì* in your body.
6. If you have an image of the White Tiger, use any preferred method of smell concentration gnosis to charge it with your intent to cultivate personal *yì*.
7. You may also ask the White Tiger to share any insights he has with you. After you are finished communicating with him, thank him and send him on his way.

Banishing:
Banish with laughter. Relight your incense any time you feel it is necessary. Carry your image of the White Tiger to enhance personal *yì* and increase vigilance.

Water: Ancestor Veneration

Ceremonially honoring deceased ancestors is a long-held Chinese esoteric practice. It typically involves offering them food and drink (Scott, 2007), burning incense offerings (Feng & Du, 2015; Wen, 2016), and burning spirit money (Blake, 2011; Scott, 2007). Paper offerings resembling gold bars, personal items, clothes, electronics, cigarettes, credit cards, and more may also be burned. Specific procedures for burning paper are typically decided by individual practitioners, but it is widely believed the paper must be burned completely to cross over into the spirit world (Scott, 2007).

Many varieties of spirit money are available. Collectively, they serve a wide variety of purposes and may be directed towards different recipients. Hell money is offered to ghosts and ancestors, and is often burned alongside paper offerings resembling gold bars (Scott, 2007). Hell money resembles genuine currency, but is clearly not. It typically features an image of *Yù Dì*, the Jade Emperor, in place of the portrait on the genuine currency. The Jade Emperor oversees all realms of existence in the Daoist paradigm (Wen, 2016). Hell money typically comes in large denominations, as it is commonly used to pay for the release of souls (Scott, 2007). This is not cheap.

Here, we will venerate our ancestors. The water phase embodies *yīn* energy and the world of the dead, whereas the world of the living embodies *yáng* energy (Wen, 2016). We will offer our ancestors incense, food, drink, and Hell money. When we get to know them well, they may give us blessings or offer us counsel. The overall rite format is inspired by *Burning Money: The Material Spirit of the Chinese Lifeworld* (Blake, 2011).

Materials:
You will need a white cloth for use as an altar cloth, matches, two candles (red or white), a plate of food, a glass of water, a stick incense of your choosing in a holder, Hell money, and a cauldron or other fireproof container in which to burn your paper offerings. Photographs or personal items belonging to deceased relatives, additional paper offerings, and a firecracker are optional.

Preparation:
Place your altar cloth on a table or other flat surface facing north. Place the candles in the north corners of the table. The incense, Hell money, and cauldron should also be placed somewhere on the altar. You may also adorn your altar with photographs and personal items of deceased relatives, additional paper offerings, and anything else you feel is important. Leave a space in the center of the table for the food and glass of water.

Statement of Intent:
It is my will to venerate my ancestors.

Procedure:
1. Light the candles to attract your ancestors. Visualize a gate to the afterlife opening between the candles. Light the incense and bow towards the gate three times. Say:

   Venerable ancestors, known and unknown,
   I will to honor you!
   I offer you these candles
   emitting light, heat, and energy!
   I offer you this incense
   that carries my good will and respect!

> **Venerable ancestors, known and unknown,
> I will for you to join me!**

2. Continue visualizing the gate between the two candles. Ancestors will walk up to this gate. Some you may know, and some you may not. See them in your mind's eye as clearly as you can. You may converse with them if you'd like. Tell them how much you miss them, or tell them the latest family news. Note that in many lineages it is considered rude to make specific requests of your ancestors the first few times you meet.

3. Place the food and glass of water on your altar. You are offering it to your ancestors, so do not consume any of it. Say:

> **I offer you this food and drink
> so you may consume its essence!**

4. Ignite the Hell money and place it in your cauldron. You may also burn any additional paper offerings you have at this time. Visualize the smoke from the offerings going through the gate and received by your ancestors. Say:

> **I offer you this Hell money
> for use in the afterlife!**

5. After the paper offerings have been consumed completely by the fire, bow to your ancestors three times.

Banishing:
Say:

> **Venerable ancestors, known and unknown,
> I willed to honor you!
> Depart peacefully now through the gates**

carrying my good will and respect!
Venerable ancestors, known and unknown,
I thank you for joining me!

Strongly visualize your ancestors walking back into the afterlife with your gifts. Light a small firecracker (away from people, pets, etc.) to end the rite. The firecracker will banish any spirits in the area. If you are in a place where firecrackers are not practical or are altogether prohibited, loudly clap your hands and banish with laughter instead.

Scatter the ashes outside. Bury the food or place it outside. Pour the water on the ground outside or into naturally occurring running water. Do not consume the food and drink offered to the dead – it is filled with *yīn* energy. It is believed that consuming them will make you feel weak, drained, and bring misfortune.

Chapter 9 Homework

After taking notes on the chapter, magical practice should be commenced for a minimum of 30 minutes each day for the remainder of the month. Perform the assignments in the order presented. Remember to document your efforts in your magical diary.

1. Meditate on the five phases in the context of Daoist cosmology. How do they affect your life? How do you interact with them?
2. Compare and contrast the western and Buddhist elements with the five phases. How do cosmological differences shape perception and interaction with the elements in each of these paradigms?
3. Meditate on the Confucian virtues of *rén*, *lǐ*, and *yì*. How do they manifest in your life? Which ones would you like to cultivate further? Determine how

balancing the five phases can facilitate this process, and take tangible steps to follow through.

4. Meditate on the associations for each phase. Then, "think in fives" to discover their underlying rationale. You may also rearrange any traditional associations to suit your personal practice if necessary.

5. Meditate on the sequence of phases in the *xiāngshēng* [mutual generation] and *xiāngkè* [mutual conquest] cycles. How does each phase interact with the others in them? What other sequences or cycles can you think of? Additional cycles can be found at *Wandering Dao* (http://wanderingdao.com/five-elements-cycles/).

6. Revisit your health and wellbeing, but this time from a traditional Chinese medicine perspective. Do your physical and mental states suggest the five phases are out of balance? If so, how? Determine what practical steps you can take to improve your body and mind, and then follow through. It is generally more effective to start with a few small changes and then work up to larger ones. If you are unsure where to start, consult with a licensed nutritionist or physician.

7. Perform the chaos magic-inspired rites to experience the Chinese phases. They are intentionally sequenced to reflect the *xiāngshēng* [mutual generation] cycle.

Chapter 10
Creating Your Own
Elemental Rites

Magical Rite Components

Belief is a tool no different than any other. However, randomly throwing components together and haphazardly following through with a rite rarely achieves results. Effective magical rites require a solid foundation and the "nuts and bolts" of a working to be sound. As long as the key components that make magic work are intact, you can obtain quality results regardless of the paradigm you are using. Some crucial things to keep in mind are discussed point-by-point below.

Statement of Intent:
A statement of intent is your confident declaration of what you will to happen immediately before performing the rite. A basic format you may follow is "It is my will to _____." State the desired result as literally and as plainly as possible. Avoid use of idiomatic and colloquial language. Years ago, I declared it was my will to "run into" a long-lost friend. I indeed met my long-lost friend, as I desired, but we almost crashed into each other when our brakes malfunctioned at the same time!

Results will manifest through the path of least resistance. If you are not specific enough the desired outcome might vaguely happen, but if you are too explicit it may be difficult for the universe to manifest a result within the confines of your specifications. Many magicians

I know have stories of willing to obtain a large sum of money, performing their rite, and then obtaining that large sum of money via an inheritance when a beloved relative died shortly thereafter. Automobile and work accidents are other unfortunate variations.

Means to Gnosis:
The method of gnosis should be consistent with the paradigm and purpose of your rite. For example, if it is your will to evoke an undine, doing so by gazing into a candle flame is not a good choice. Gazing into a dish of cool liquid would be more appropriate, as it is more consistent with the nature of elemental water. On the other hand, if it is your will to evoke a sylph, gazing into a pot of dirt is not a good choice. Chanting into incense smoke would be more appropriate, as it is more consistent with the nature of elemental air.

Although more than one method of gnosis can be incorporated into a rite, simpler is generally better, especially when you are just starting out. After you are comfortable writing and performing simpler rites that achieve decent results, feel free to create more complex, layered rites that incorporate multiple methods of gnosis. If this is something you are interested in, it is usually easier to perform an inhibitory before an excitatory method. The other way around doesn't work as efficiently.

Gnosis:
Achieving an altered state of consciousness allows your desire to penetrate into your subconscious mind, where it can be uploaded into the universe. Even if you do not achieve gnosis the desired results may still manifest if the other components of your rite are technically sound. Typically, the more frequently you achieve gnosis the easier it is to reach again. Some methods may yield an altered state of consciousness easily, while others you will have to work for. Though the most

effective forms of gnosis vary widely among individuals, don't get stuck on using only one method.

What will you do in the rite when you achieve gnosis? This varies widely and depends on the purpose of the rite, the elements you are working with, and many other factors. For an earth element rite aimed at producing wealth you could charge a lucky coin to keep in your pocket while visualizing your bank account balance increasing. For an air element rite aimed at making you a more effective speaker you could invoke an eloquent egregore and then anchor that mental state to a word, gesture, laser pointer, or something else. For a water element rite aimed at healing someone you could ritually wash the illness away from a poppet representing him or her. For a fire element rite aimed at banishing a specific target you could throw a symbolic representation of the target into a bonfire and then dance around in celebration of said banishment. The possibilities are endless!

Forget It:

After performing your rite, document your efforts in your magical diary and then do your best to forget it. Detaching from your desire will prevent "lust of result" from short-circuiting its manifestation. The more you dwell on your desire the more difficult it will be for the universe to shift probability in your favor and produce the desired outcome. An alternate way to look at it is when you dwell on your rite, you are stealing energy from it that could otherwise be directed towards manifesting the result.

Types of Magic

Magical operations may be broadly classified into one of five categories: invocation, evocation, divination, enchantment, and illumination (Carroll, 1987). Some rites use only one modality, while more complex ones may combine many. Each operation is discussed point-by-point below.

Invocation:
Invocation can be defined as bringing an external energy or vibration inside of you. Alternatively, some magicians perceive invocation as peeling away psychological layers to reveal hidden aspects lying dormant in your psyche. Generally, invocations vary according to the thing invoked, the nature of the paradigm, and the person doing the invoking. Looking across multiple conventional and pop culture paradigms the experience of invocation varies heavily. With some egregores invocation feels like a "trust fall," while with others it feels like being ridden by a Vodoun *loa*.

Some egregores are pleasant to work with, and others not so much. Sometimes this is challenging to predict. For example, on the surface Hello Kitty appears to be a benign, happy cat. However, she has a domineering "You will love me and be happy whether you want to or not!" attitude, as she is the most popular Sanrio character. Most "big bank" egregores are not pleasant at all. University mascots tend to be hit or miss.

Before invoking an entity of interest determine as many correspondences as you can. Research the entity's personality, talents, likes, dislikes, catch phrases, etc. as much as possible. These crucial pieces of data will aid in the design of your invocation. With each entity you choose put lots of thought in beforehand and make sure your methods are consistent with its nature. If you've never previously performed an invocation it is highly recommended you gain some experience using conventional (as opposed to pop culture) paradigms first so you have some idea of what to expect.

Evocation:
In evocation you are bringing an energy or vibration outside, instead of bringing it inside as with invocation. Many of the aforementioned invocation concepts apply. If hesitant to invoke a godform, egregore, pop culture character, or anything else, consider doing an evocation instead. This will allow you to become accustomed to the energies involved. If you look at evocations across paradigms many have the same core components. They often involve flattering the entity, offering it things it likes, and then flattering it some more.

Divination:
Divination allows you to extend your perception. Divinatory systems can be broadly classified as "active" or "passive." In "active" forms of divination you are shuffling cards, tossing coins, or otherwise manipulating objects that represent a mini-universe. In "passive" divination, such as astrology, you aren't manipulating objects that are a microcosmic representation of the universe – you are passively observing them instead. Divination systems vary widely, but whatever system you create must have clear components. A non-exhaustive list of things to consider when creating your own divination system is as follows:

1. Will your system be "active" or "passive"? Does it matter?
2. What elements, archetypes, or aspects of the universe will each card, rock, cereal marshmallow, or whatever represent? How "complete" is this representation of the universe in your paradigm of choice? Is it necessary to completely represent it?
3. What types of questions will your system answer? In other words, will it produce a yes/no response, tell a story, give timeframes, give a combination of these things, or something else?

4. What are the strengths and weaknesses of your system? What are its limitations?
5. What will you say or do before/during/after your divination? Will you recite a prayer, gaze at something, shuffle something, toss something, pour milk into a cereal bowl, or something else?
6. Is your system completely novel, or is it comparable (archetypally or mechanistically) to aspects of other, well-established systems (such as astrology, Tarot, runes, *yìjīng*, reading tealeaves...)?

Enchantment:

When you perform an enchantment, you are imposing your will on the universe to make stuff happen. As T. S. Eliot stated, "...Runes and charms are very practical formulae designed to produce definite results, such as getting a cow out of a bog" (1943/2009, p. 22). The means to your desired end may involve the use of sigils, charms, talismans, runes, *mantras*, *mudrās*, cards, poppets, or other assorted magical items. The elemental tools you created in the previous chapters may also play a role in your enchantments.

There are many ways enchantment may be accomplished. This topic will not be addressed in depth here, as it has been extensively discussed in the occult literature. A non-exhaustive list of things to consider when creating an enchantment is as follows:

1. Is the "stuff" you will to happen represented in the paradigm your enchantment will be performed in?
2. What magical items are appropriate to use, and what are their roles in the paradigm the enchantment will be performed in?
3. What forms of gnosis are suitable for your enchantment? Are they consistent with the purpose of your rite and the system you are using?

4. What will you do with your magical items after gnosis? After the rite is finished?

Illumination:
Illumination involves objective introspection void of delusion. It facilitates contemplation and metamorphosis of the self so you may take your place in the universe and work harmoniously with it. Much of your previous homework involved illumination in the form of elemental meditations. You also performed introspection to determine which virtues and vices associated with a particular temperament you have, and then took concrete steps to edit your personality to your liking.

Illumination deals with wisdom – acquiring knowledge and applying it properly. It is "going meta" and becoming aware of the causes and effects of your actions, instead of blindly following through. It is busting through illusion to become more aware of yourself, others, and situations. It can help you reveal hidden variables in a situation or discover hidden options that do not immediately reveal themselves. It may be achieved through mechanisms of invocation, evocation, divination, enchantment, and various amalgamations thereof.

Example Group Rites

Example group rites inspired by the elements are outlined below. They have been performed numerous times and all yielded decent results (see Appendix C). Feel free to modify them to your liking.

Serafim Disco Inferno

In *The Bible* Isaiah has a vision of the *Serafim* circling *YHWH* on the throne (Isaiah 6:1-13, *King James Bible*). They each have six wings – two cover their faces, two cover their feet, and two are used for flying. Isaiah states he is woeful because his lips are unclean. In response a member of these angelic choirs use tongs to pick up a piece of burning coal from the altar. The coal touches Isaiah's mouth, removing his guilt and atoning for his sins.

Here, we will purify ourselves by reenacting Isaiah's vision using hot peppers instead of coals. I typically use habaneros, but anything spicy will work. Evoking *YHWH* also evokes the *Serafim*. With the *Serafim* present we will bite into the hot peppers and disco dance. The gnosis is from exhaustion (via dancing) and spicy food. If the latter is disagreeable to you it is possible to just lick the pepper or hold it to your lips without tasting it and still obtain quality results.

Materials:
You will need hot peppers (one per person), materials to make a triangle, "Disco Inferno" by The Trammps, and a gaudy crucifix.

Preparation:
Make a triangle on the ground that is large enough to hold the hot peppers and gaudy crucifix. Participants should stand outside the triangle, as *YHWH* and the *Serafim* will be evoked into it.

Statement of Intent:
It is our will for the *Serafim* to purify us.

Procedure:
1. Each participant should meditate on the vices they want to be rid of. (Optional: Use a controlled, fixed spin to bring the vices to the surface of your consciousness.)

2. Evoke *YHWH* – the *Serafim* will follow. Say:

YHWH, we evoke you
from the limitless light!

Surrounded by *Serafim*,
perpetually in flight!
We command you, Burning Ones,
to purify our souls.
We offer you these hot peppers
for use like Isaiah's coals!

3. Participants should chant *Serafim*... *Serafim*... *Serafim*... until they are evoked.
4. Visualize the *Serafim* imbuing the hot peppers with elemental fire. Each person should then grab a hot pepper.
5. Start the music, bite into the hot pepper, and disco dance until the song is over. Visualize the heat from the pepper burning away your vices.

6. After the song ends, dismiss the *Serafim*:

Our lips burn hot with purity
scorching away our negativity.
We dismiss you, *Serafim*, blazing angelic choirs.
We thank you for your cleansing fire!

Banishing:
Banish with laughter.

Lucky Charms

General Mills, Inc., is an American multinational manufacturer and marketer of various foods sold at retail stores. Lucky Charms, which debuted in the 1960s, is a product of General Mills and was the first cereal to contain marshmallows. The first version of the cereal had four marshmallows – pink hearts, yellow moons, orange stars, and green clovers. The marshmallows represent Lucky the Leprechaun's magical charms.

The lineup of marshmallows has changed over time, but the original four correlate well with the Aristotelian elements. The heart charm corresponds to fire, the star charm to air, the moon charm to water, and the clover charm to earth. Each marshmallow charm has its own unique power, described on the *Lucky Charms Official Website* (http://www.luckycharms. com/) and *Tumblr* (http://luckycharms.tumblr.com/). The current incarnations of the original four marshmallow charms are: pink heart, grants the power to bring things to "life;" yellow (now blue) moon, grants the power of "invisibility;" orange (now "shooting") star, grants the power of "flight;" and green clover, grants the power of "luck."

In the earliest commercials Lucky Charms had no theme jingle, but it soon became "Frosted Lucky Charms, / they're magically delicious!" The cereal's mascot is Lucky the Leprechaun, who first appeared in 1964. In this paradigm only leprechauns are allowed to use the charms. Here, we will evoke Lucky the Leprechaun and compel "General Mills" (the General Mills, Inc. egregore) to flog him so we can use the "Lucky Charms" for ourselves.

Materials:
You will need St. Patrick's Day paraphernalia (to make a triangle), an image of the General Mills, Inc. logo, a flogger (for "General Mills"), a leprechaun hat (for Lucky), bowls of Lucky Charms cereal, and craft supplies (to make permanent "lucky charms"). Spicy food is optional.

Gnosis:
"General Mills" and Lucky the Leprechaun may use any preferred method. The gnosis for other participants in each "lucky charm" group is: heart charm, chanting and (optional) spicy food; moon charm, spinning (a slow, controlled spin); star charm, glossolalia; and clover charm, chanting and trying to not laugh.

Preparation:

Divine which marshmallow charm will benefit each participant the most, using any preferred method. Each participant should create a permanent "lucky charm" craft representing his or her divined marshmallow.

Make a triangle on the floor with the St. Patrick's Day paraphernalia that is large enough to hold the two volunteers, the lucky charm crafts, and any extra cereal (Figure 10.1). One volunteer will invoke Lucky the Leprechaun, and the other the General Mills, Inc. egregore. The volunteer invoking "General Mills" should hold the company logo and flogger. The volunteer invoking Lucky the Leprechaun should wear the leprechaun hat.

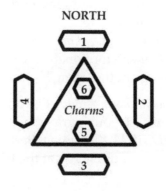

NORTH

Figure 10.1. Lucky Charms rite setup. The charms, any additional cereal, and St. Patrick's Day paraphernalia should be placed inside the triangle. Locations of the various "lucky charm" groups and invocants are: 1, clover charm group; 2, star charm group; 3, heart charm group; 4, moon charm group; 5, "General Mills"; and 6, Lucky the Leprechaun.

Statement of Intent:

It is our will to lead a charmed life.

Procedure:

The volunteer invoking "General Mills" may use any preferred method involving the General Mills, Inc. logo. After "General Mills" is present, all participants should evoke Lucky the Leprechaun while the volunteer dressed as Lucky invokes. The evocation is:

> **Lucky the Leprechaun, we evoke thee!**
> **Grant us your marshmallow charms!**
> **You, borne of General Mills, Inc. in 1963,**
> **we evoke thee!**
> **Grant us your marshmallow charms!**
> **Frosted Lucky Charms, they're magically delicious!**
> **Grant us your marshmallow charms!**

"General Mills" can start flogging Lucky the Leprechaun as soon as Lucky is present. This will compel Lucky to enchant the charms, cereal, and any other items in the triangle.

Participants outside the triangle should reach gnosis via the assigned methods. Group assignments are determined by the charm divined. The *mantras* serve to keep Lucky in the triangle and charge the charms. Means to gnosis for each group are:

Heart charm group: Vibrate **HRĪḤ** from your Solar Plexus *cakra* with (optional) spicy food in your mouth. Direct your energy at the triangle.

Moon charm group: Perform a controlled, fixed spin and contract your aura while whispering, **XIQUAL BICOW ODIBUM** [Ouranian Barbaric: Manifest in the triangle]. Direct your energy at the triangle.

Star charm group: Visualize yourself as an orange shooting star and chant **GOKCHOSOD OXO KICFAV** [Bless our items] into glossolalia. Direct your energy at the triangle.

Clover charm group: Stuff your face with cereal while exclaiming, "**They're magically delicious!**" towards the triangle over and over. Try to not laugh.

"General Mills" should flog Lucky for as long as necessary. After Lucky has enchanted the charms, cereal, and anything else inside the triangle, he may be dismissed.

Banishing:
Banish with laughter. Enjoy your charm!

Gaṇeśa Stomp

Gaṇeśa is the elephant-headed deity revered in the Hindu pantheon. He is the lord of new beginnings, dweller of the threshold, and creator/remover of obstacles in our lives (Grimes, 1995). He is commonly depicted with four arms, an elephant's head, and a plump belly. His broken tusk is the focal point of many legends (see Krishnaswami, 1996). He is commonly depicted holding a trident, an axe, rope, his broken tusk, or other symbolic items.

Gaṇeśa also bears elemental significance, as he embodies the great elements of the Hindu and Buddhist paradigms. His iconography parallels the *stūpa*. The base he sits upon represents earth, his plump, circular belly represents water, his triangular face represents fire, a crescent (his Third Eye) represents air, and his flame represents space (Grimes, 1995).

In his role as Lord of Obstacles he inserts or removes obstacles in our lives. Here, we will invoke *Gaṇeśa* to overcome obstacles. We will write our obstacles on index cards and then invoke him. Then, we will stomp on the cards like elephants to squash our obstacles. The rite will culminate in burning the index cards. The gnosis is chanting or pain from stomping really hard.

Materials:
You will need markers, index cards, matches, a cauldron (or other flame-resistant container), and sandalwood or *nag champa* incense sticks (one per participant). Indian drumming music is optional.

Preparation:
Place the cauldron in the center of the room. Everyone should write obstacles they'd like to overcome on the index cards. Obstacles can be material, psychological, or spiritual. Aim for one obstacle per card. Repeat obstacles from different people are okay. Scatter the cards around

the cauldron in a circle. Everyone will be stomping on the cards during the rite.

Statement of Intent:
It is our will to overcome obstacles.

Procedure:
Everyone gather round the cauldron in a circle, standing on the cards. Make sure there is enough distance between participants for everyone to safely stomp around. Light your incense sticks. Extend your arms in front of you, still holding the incense stick, so as to resemble an elephant's trunk. One person may lead the invocation, while the other participants repeat after. Say:

> *Gaṇeśa,* **Lord of Obstacles,**
> **we invoke you!**
> **One-Tusked One**
> **who embodies the finite and the infinite,**
> **the five great elements,**
> **we invoke you!**
> **Lend us your wisdom**
> **so we may overcome obstacles,**
> **both seen and unseen!**
> **Lord** *Gaṇapati,*
> **whose belly contains the universe**
> **and whose word is** *OM,*
> **we invoke you!**

Start the (optional) music. Visualize yourself as *Gaṇeśa* while holding your incense stick with both arms in front of you, like an elephant's trunk. Stomp on the cards while moving counterclockwise around the cauldron. As you raise each foot, stomp it down forcefully and with intent as an elephant would. Chant *OM* while stomping. After everyone has stomped on the cards for at least 10 minutes, place them in the cauldron. Say:

We embody the wisdom of *Gaṇeśa,*
the finite and the infinite,
the five great elements!
We create our own universe
and have the power
to squash our obstacles,
both seen and unseen!

Burn the cards while chanting **OṂ**. Dispose of the ashes in water or by burying them.

Banishing:
Banish with laughter. Relight your incense stick any time you feel it is necessary.

Chapter 10 Homework

After taking notes on the chapter, magical practice should be commenced for a minimum of 30 minutes each day for the remainder of the month. Perform the assignments in the order presented. Remember to document your efforts in your magical diary.

1. Meditate on the types of magic (invocation, evocation, divination, enchantment, and illumination) for a minimum of 10 minutes each day. What is each type useful for? Are different types better suited towards particular elements?
2. Create and perform an elemental invocation rite. For example, you may invoke a godform, egregore, or pop culture character that embodies elemental qualities you would like to integrate into your personality.
3. Create and perform an elemental evocation rite. For example, you may evoke a godform, egregore, or pop culture character that bears elemental significance, and then charge it with a task

complementary to its personality and the element.

4. Perform a divination to determine the influence of each element on your life, in ranked order. You may use an existing divination system or create your own. For example, I created a divination system using Lucky Charms marshmallows. Upright marshmallows indicate positive elemental influences, whereas upside-down marshmallows indicate negative ones. It can reveal what elements are at play in a person or situation, as well as their ranked order of influence.

5. Create and perform an elemental enchantment rite. For example, I enchanted five different hairclips – one for each western element. Each hairclip conferred a beneficial characteristic consistent with that element's nature when worn.

6. Create and perform an elemental illumination rite. It may be something simple, such as a guided meditation to promote elemental balance, or it may be more complex, such as a layered rite to obtain wisdom and guidance from aether.

7. Examine the overall structure of the example rites. Performing them is optional. What did you like and dislike about each one? What would you change?

Chapter 11
Final Thoughts

You made it! You have successfully worked with each classical western element, gained insight into eastern elements, and performed numerous elemental rites. You also have the tools to write your own. If you have been working at the suggested pace of no more than one chapter per month, this is your 11th month or more.

Where Do We Go from Here?

You can go anywhere you want. The elements are yours to use. Revisit them. Explore them in new paradigms of your choosing. Use them to facilitate health, harmony, and life balance. Use them in entirely novel ways that no one has imagined yet. Go nuts with the Periodic Table. Whatever you choose keep in mind Lévi's Four Powers of the Sphinx: to know, to will, to dare, and to keep silent. These magical virtues are traditionally associated with elemental air, fire, water, and earth, respectively (Crowley, 1909/1999). "...It is necessary to KNOW what has to be done, to WILL what is required, to DARE what must be attempted and to KEEP SILENT with discernment" (Lévi, 1898/2000, p. 40). Strive to maintain balance among them to reach your highest potential.

To Know:

Know thyself.

–Delphic maxim

The above phrase was inscribed over the entrance of the Temple of Apollo at Delphi in ancient Greece (Pausanias, 10.24.1, trans. 1918). Introspection has provided you with two unbiased occult mirrors of yourself – one reflects your virtues, and the other your vices. Update them regularly to maintain their accuracy. Know that you are not the same person as when you began this work. The elements have changed you in a way only attainable through direct experience. You have also learned that your personality is mutable and have taken steps to edit it to your liking. Drawing upon elemental air will give you the perspective needed to identify your gaps in knowledge and then fill them. Be lighthearted and lucid, like air at its best.

To Will:

In the absence of will power, the most complete collection of virtues and talents is wholly worthless.

–Aleister Crowley

Crowley wrote this in regard to two students who strengthened his conviction on the importance of willpower (quoted in Mistlberger, 2020, p. 243). The note-taking and homework in each chapter have facilitated development of your focus, resolution, and discipline – key ingredients for a strong Will. Maintain it through enthusiastic, consistent practice. Drawing upon elemental fire will enhance your drive and determination. Will what is required to achieve your goals. If your will is strong enough, you will find a way. Otherwise, you will find an excuse. When you are carrying out your True Will you will have the momentum of the universe behind you. Be brave and tenacious, like fire at its best.

To Dare:

Life is either a daring adventure or nothing.
To keep our faces toward change and behave like free spirits in the presence of fate is strength undefeatable.

–Helen Keller

The above statement appears in Helen Keller's *Let Us Have Faith* (quoted in Shapiro, 2006, p. 418). Here, you dared to practice the art and science of magic to commune with the elements on a deeper level. This is just the beginning. For each success you will have many failures, but that is inevitable when you are doing something new and different. Don't give up. I've been practicing magic since childhood, and can't even begin to count how many epic, idiotic mistakes I've made. Dare to be true to yourself, and dare to change your universe. Drawing upon elemental water will give you the guts to dream big, even when you are absolutely terrified. Be imaginative and compassionate, like water at its best.

To Keep Silent:

> *Never miss a good chance to shut up.*
> –Will Rogers

Will Rogers was an American actor and social commentator (quoted in Cullen, 2006, p. 955). Though not directly addressed here you have experienced the virtue of silence (or lack thereof) throughout your elemental journey. Be circumspect. Do not be a braggart. Stay humble. Your actions will speak louder than your words. Do not indiscriminately share personal information, especially regarding your magical interests. In some societies the practice of magic may still result in negative consequences if you are discovered. Besides, the more silent you are, the more observant you will become. Then the elements will reveal themselves to you even more. Enjoy the silence. Be cautious, steady, and humble, like earth at its best.

Ready, Set, Go!

Lévi (1898/2000) continues, "When one does not know, one should will to learn. To the extent that one does not know it is foolhardy to dare, but it is always well to keep silent" (p. 41). The elemental forces recur in many paradigms. If you would like to more deeply explore them in a particular tradition, a short list of recommended books can be found in the following pages. Some focus entirely on the elements, while others have a specific section dedicated to them. They are available in most major bookstores or online. The list is by no means complete. There are many excellent books (and entire paradigms!) that are not included for brevity's sake.

Buddhism:

Bhikkhu, T. (Trans.). (1997). *Dhatu-vibhanga Sutta: An Analysis of the Properties* (MN 140). Available at http://www.accesstoinsight.org/tipitaka/mn/mn.140.than.html

Bhikkhu, T. (Trans.). (2003). *Maha-hatthipadopama Sutta: The Great Elephant Footprint Simile* (MN 28). Available at http://www.accesstoinsight.org/tipitaka/mn/mn.028.than.html

Thurman, R. A. F. (Trans.). (1994). *The Tibetan Book of the Dead: Liberation Through Understanding the In Between.* New York, NY: Bantam Books.

Ceremonial magic:

Crowley, A. (1999). *777 Revised.* In I. Regardie (Ed.), *777 and Other Qabalistic Writings of Aleister Crowley.* York Beach, ME: Weiser Books. (Original work published 1909)

Kraig, D. M. (2010). *Modern Magick: Twelve Lessons in the High Magickal Arts* (Rev.). St. Paul, MN: Llewellyn Publications.

Whitcomb, B. (2004). *The Magician's Companion: An Encyclopedic and Practical Guide to Magical Symbolism.* St. Paul, MN: Llewellyn Publications.

Chinese Cosmology:

Wang, A. (2000). *Cosmology and Political Culture in Early China.* Cambridge, United Kingdom: Cambridge University Press.

Daoism:

Wen, B. (2016). *The Tao of Craft: Fu Talismans and Casting Sigils in the Eastern Esoteric Tradition.* Berkeley, CA: North Atlantic Books.

Druidry:

Wolfe, A. (2005). *Druid Power: Celtic Faerie Craft & Elemental Magic.* St Paul, MN: Llewellyn Publications.

Greek Cosmology:

Arikha, N. (2007). *Passions and Tempers: A History of the Humours.* New York, NY: Ecco.

P. Curd (Ed.). (2011). *A Presocratics Reader: Selected Fragments and Testimonia* (2nd ed.). (R. D. McKirahan and P. Curd, Trans.). Indianapolis, IN: Hackett Publishing Company.

Hermetics:

Bardon, F. (trans. 2001). *Initiation into Hermetics* (G. Hanswille & F. Gallo, Trans.). Salt Lake City, UT: Merkur Publishing. (Original work published 1956)

Bardon, F. (trans. 2001). *The Practice of Magical Evocation* (G. Hanswille & F. Gallo, Trans.). Salt Lake City, UT: Merkur Publishing. (Original work published 1956)

Soror Velchanes

Hinduism:

Chāndogya Upaniṣad. (trans. 1996). In *Upaniṣads* (P. Olivelle, Trans.). Oxford, England: Oxford University Press.

Yogatattva Upaniṣad. (trans. 1914). In *Thirty Minor Upaniṣads* (K. N. Ayar, Trans.). Available at http://www.sacred-texts.com/hin/tmu/tmu25.htm

Paganism:

Conway, D. J. (2005). *Elemental Magick: Meditations, Exercises, Spells, and Rituals to Help You Connect with Nature.* Franklin Lakes, NJ: New Page Books.

Cunningham, S. (1997). *Earth Power: Techniques of Natural Magic.* St. Paul, MN: Llewellyn Publications.

Cunningham, S. (1999). *Earth, Air, Water, & Fire: More Techniques of Natural Magic.* St. Paul, MN: Llewellyn Publications.

Wicca:

Lipp, D. (2004). *The Way of Four: Create Elemental Balance in Your Life.* St. Paul, MN: Llewellyn Publications.

Lipp, D. (2006). *The Way of Four Spellbook: Working Magic with the Elements.* St. Paul, MN: Llewellyn Publications.

Appendix A
The *Qabala*

The *Qabala* [Heb. קבלה] is a cornerstone of the western esoteric tradition. It is a way of reception (of the nature of the universe) and revelation. Studying it will help you place your elemental work in a greater context. Overall, the *Qabala* may be classified into five parts, which are as follows. They are not mutually exclusive.

1. *Oral.* Received through word of mouth, such as receiving instruction from a teacher.
2. *Written.* Received through reading books about *Qabala* or books written from a *Qabalistic* perspective on some other topic. It is traditionally aimed at explaining the form and function of the universe.
3. *Literal.* Received through reading holy books and examining them for *Qabalistic* insight, especially via *gematria*, *temura*, and *notariqon*. *Gematria* involves examining the numerical attributes of Hebrew letters to discover new relationships among words. *Temura* involves changing letters in sentences to form new ones. *Notariqon* produces new words (such as acronyms) or sentences from permuting others.
4. *Symbolic.* Concerned with understanding the *Qabala*, the self, and universe through studying symbols, especially the *Tree of Life*.
5. *Practical.* Applying the *Qabala* to cause internal or external change. Esoteric and magical application of the *Qabala* falls under this category. This category often includes aspects of the other four.

The wisdom of the *Qabala* can be summarized into one glyph, the *Tree of Life* (Figure A1), which we first saw in Chapter 1. Its 10 spheres and 22 paths represent specific archetypal forces, many of which bear direct or indirect elemental significance. A complete *Tree of Life* exists in the four worlds: 'Aṣilut [Heb. Archetypal World], Beri'a [Creative World], Yeṣiraḥ [Formative World], and 'Asiya [Material World]. Each world represents a different aspect of the unfolding of creation and corresponds to a particular element as well as a letter of the Tetragrammaton [Heb. יהוה], the proper four-letter name of the God of Israel.

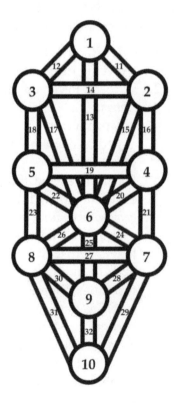

Figure A1. The Qabalistic *Tree of Life.* Spheres and paths are labeled with key numbers. Paths 31 and 32 have dual attributes, which are referred to as 31-*bis* and 32-*bis*, respectively. See Tables A1 and A2 for additional information.

The Spheres

The 10th sphere, *Malkut*, is the realm of the elements and where we focused much of our attention throughout this workbook. Basic attributes of each sphere are shown in Table A1. Queen Scale colors are also given because they frequently appear in the occult literature and because they efficiently reveal relationships among the spheres via their color correspondence relationships.

Spheres 1, 2, and 3 are the Supernal Triad of transpersonal, incomprehensible states. The Abyss is an imaginary horizontal line separating the Supernal Triad from the rest of the tree. Spheres 4 and 5 represent the soul. Sphere 6 is the personal self (the "I"). Spheres 7, 8, 9, and 10 make up our personality.

The spheres reside on one of three vertical pillars. The left pillar, composed of *Bina, Gebura,* and *Hod,* is the Pillar of Severity. It represents universal form. The right pillar, composed of *Ḥakma, Ḥesed,* and *Neṣaḥ,* is the Pillar of Mercy. It represents universal force. The middle pillar is the Pillar of Balance, composed of *Keter, Tif'eret, Yesod,* and *Malkut.* It represents equilibration (form and force in balance) and consciousness.

The Paths

Each path connects two spheres together, equilibrating them. The paths are named after the 22 Hebrew consonants. Basic attributes of each path are shown in Table A2. If you would like to make a colored image for your notes, Queen Scale colors are also given.

Table A1. *Spheres of the* Qabala

Key No.	Sphere	English Meaning	Aspect of Self	Queen Scale Color
1	כתר [Keter]	Crown	Pure spirit of transpersonal self	White brilliance
2	חכמה [Hakma]	Wisdom	Transpersonal will & purpose	Gray
3	בינה [Bina]	Understanding	Transpersonal love & awareness	Black
4	חסד [Hesed]	Love	Personal love and awareness	Blue
5	גבורה [Gebura]	Strength	Personal will and power	Scarlet red
6	תפארת [Tif eret]	Beauty	Personal self (the "I") and pure self awareness	Yellow (or gold)
7	נצח [Nesah]	Victory	Inner feelings (e.g. love, hate, joy, sadness)	Emerald green
8	הוד [Hod]	Splendor	The intellectual mind, thoughts, communication	Orange
9	יסוד [Yesod]	Foundation	Unconscious mind, serves as a conduit for the higher self and drives us to fulfill our needs	Violet (or silver)
10	מלכות [Malkut]	Kingdom	Physical body, material world of the five senses, & realm of the terrestrial elements	Citrine (a yellow), olive green, russet (a red), and black

Information is adapted from Crowley (1909/1999), Kaplan (Trans.) (1997), and personal notes.

Table A2. *Paths of the* Qabala

Key Number	Path	Letter Meaning	Romanization[a]	Queen Scale Color
11	א [ˈalef]	Ox	' or omitted	Sky blue
12	ב [bet]	House	b or v	Purple
13	ג [gimel]	Camel	g	Silver
14	ד [dalet]	Door	d	Sky blue
15	ה [he]	Window	h	Red
16	ו [waw]	Nail	w	Deep indigo
17	ז [zayin]	Sword	z	Pale mauve (a purple)
18	ח [ḥet]	Fence	ḥ	Maroon (a red)
19	ט [ṭet]	Serpent	ṭ	Deep purple
20	י [yod]	Hand	y	Slate gray
21	כ [kaf]	Palm of hand	k	Blue
22	ל [lamed]	Ox-goad[b]	l	Blue
23	מ [mem]	Water	m	Sea green
24	נ [nun]	Fish	n	Dull brown
25	ס [samek]	Prop[c]	s	Yellow
26	ע [ˈayin]	Eye	' or omitted	Black
27	פ [pe]	Mouth	p or f	Red
28	צ [ṣade]	Fishhook	ṣ	Sky blue
29	ק [qof]	Back of head	q	Buff (a brown), flecked silver-white
30	ר [resh]	Head	r	Golden yellow
31[d]	ש [sin/shin]	Tooth	s or sh	Vermillion (a red)
31-*bis*				Dark purple, nearly black
32[d]	ת [taw]	Cross	t	Black
32-*bis*				Amber (a yellow-orange)

Information is adapted from Crowley (1909/1999), Kaplan (Trans.) (1997), and personal notes. Regarding the elements, 32-*bis* is attributed to earth, 11 to air, 23 to water, 31 to fire, and 31-*bis* to aether (spirit). [a]Romanization is adapted from *The SBL Handbook of Style* (Alexander et al. (Eds.), 1999). [b]An ox-goad is a pointy stick used to guide oxen. [c]A prop is a supportive object (such as a door prop used to hold it open). [d]In paths with dual attributes letter correspondences are the same, but color correspondences vary.

Further Reading

If you would like to learn more about the *Qabala* a short list of recommended books is as follows. They are available in most major bookstores or online.

Crowley, A. (1999). *777 Revised*. In I. Regardie (Ed.), *777 and Other Qabalistic Writings of Aleister Crowley*. York Beach, ME: Weiser Books. (Original work published 1909)

DuQuette, L. M. (2001). *The Chicken Qabalah of Rabbi Lamed Ben Clifford*. York Beach, ME: Weiser Books.

Fortune, D. (2000). *The Mystical Qabalah* (Rev. ed.). York Beach, ME: Weiser Books. (Original work published 1935)

Kaplan, A. (Trans.) (1997). *Sefer Yetzirah: The Book of Creation in Theory and Practice* (Rev. ed.). York Beach, ME: Weiser Books.

Parfitt, W. (1991). *The New Living Qabalah: A Practical & Experimental Guide to Understanding the Tree of Life*. Boston, MA: Element Books.

Zohar: The Book of Enlightenment. (trans. 1983). (D. C. Matt, Trans.) New York, NY: Paulist Press.

.

Appendix B
The Hebrew *Alefbet* and Divine Names

The Hebrew *alefbet* is put to use by a wide variety of magicians. Hebrew is read from right to left in horizontal lines. Biblical Hebrew lacks diacritics, so there is uncertainty as to how words were historically pronounced (Hoffman, 2004). The 22 consonants of the Biblical Hebrew *alefbet* are shown in Table B1. Going into further detail on this topic is beyond the scope of this workbook; however, if this subject interests you, there is an extensive body of scholarly literature on the evolution of Hebrew and its cognate languages (see Bodine, 1992; Hoffman, 2004; Kahn (Ed.), 2013; Young, 2003).

Try reading the two English phrases below by filling in the missing vowels where appropriate:

V GT LVLY BNCH F CCNTS
CHLDRN S MGC BCS THY LK FR T

If you fill in the vowels we obtain the phrases I'VE GOT A LOVELY BUNCH OF COCONUTS and CHILDREN SEE MAGIC BECAUSE THEY LOOK FOR IT. Biblical and modern Hebrew are written in much the same way, except they are written from right to left and are actually in Hebrew. Interpreting text in this manner is easy for native readers because they do it all the time.

Table B1. *The Hebrew* alefbet.

Letter[a]	Romanized Name[b]	IPA Pronunciation[c]
א	'alef	/ʔ/
ב	bet	/b/ or /v/
ג	gimel	/g/ or /ɣ/
ד	dalet	/d/ or /ð/
ה	he	/h/
ו	waw	/w/
ז	zayin	/z/
ח	het	/χ/ or /ħ/
ט	tet	/t/
י	yod	/j/
כ [final: ך]	kaf	/k/ or /x/
ל	lamed	/l/
מ [final: ם]	mem	/m/
נ [final: ן]	nun	/n/
ס	samek	/s/
ע	'ayin	/ɣ/ or /ʕ/
פ [final: ף]	pe	/p/ or /f/
צ [final: ץ]	sade	/ts͡/
ק	qof	/q/
ר	resh	/r/
שׁ	sin/shin	/ʃ/ or /s/
ת	taw	/t/ or /θ/

[a]Some letters have a final form that occurs only at the end of a word. [b]Romanization is adapted from *The SBL Handbook of Style* (Alexander et al. (Eds.), 1999). [c]Pronunciation is conveyed in International Phonetic Association format (2015), and is based on current understanding of Biblical Hebrew phonology (Kahn (Ed.), 2013).

Elemental Hierarchy Names

Hebrew names, Romanization (adapted from *The SBL Handbook of Style* (Alexander et al. (Eds.), 1999)), pronunciation (based on current understanding of Biblical Hebrew phonology (Kahn (Ed.), 2013)), and etymology of elemental hierarchy denizens follow in this appendix. Pronunciations, when known, are conveyed in the International Phonetic Alphabet (2015). If you want to use an alternate dialect instead, go for it. As long as you understand what you are saying, why you are saying it, and pronounce it with conviction, it should not negatively impact your magical work.

Earth

Divine name:
אדני [*Adonay* (/ʔă.d̪oˈnɔ̣i̞ː/); (my) Lord]

The name is an emphatic form of אדון [*Adon* (/ʔɔːˈd̪on̪/); n. lord] (see Strong, 1982b, #136). In Jewish traditions, it is used as a proper name of *YHWH* and spoken in place of it (Kohler, 1906a). It is the *Qabalistic* divine name associated with elemental earth (Crowley, 1909/1999).

Archangel:
אוריאל [*Uri'el* (/ʔuː.ri̞ʔel/); fire of god]

The name is a combination of אור [/ʔuːr/; n. fire] (see Strong, 1982b, #217) and אל [/ʔel/; n. god] (see #410), and is sometimes erroneously interpreted as "Light of God" (Singer & Blau, 1906). Though not named in *The Bible*, *Uri'el* is identified as an archangel in various apocryphal (e.g., *Esdras*) and pseudepigraphal texts (e.g., *The Books of Adam and Eve, Books of Enoch*…). *Uri'el* rules over the corner of the world associated with elemental earth (Agrippa, trans. 1531-1533/2004) and is the archangel of elemental earth (Crowley, 1909/1999).

Soror Velchanes

Angelic choirs:

כרובים [*Kerubim* (/ kĕˈruːbˈii̯m/)]

The singular name is written on the Seventh Pentacle of the Sun in *The Key of Solomon the King* (Mathers (Ed.), trans. 1889/2009) and identified as belonging to an elemental ruler. The root of the word is unknown in the Hebrew and Greek languages of *The Bible* (Strong, 1982a, #5502, 1982b, #3742), however cognate languages have been examined for insight (discussed in Hirsch et al., 1906). In *The Bible* they guard Eden (Genesis 3:24, *King James Bible*), as well as transport *YHWH's* throne in Ezekiel's vision (Ezekiel 10:9). Many objects, including the Ark, are decorated with their likeness (e.g., Exodus 25:18-22; 1 Kings 6:32-35; 2 Chronicles 3:7-14...). They also appear in various apocryphal (e.g., *Ecclesiasticus, Prayer of Azariah*) and pseudepigraphal texts (e.g., *The Books of Adam and Eve, Books of Enoch...*). Agrippa (trans. 1531-1533/2004) associates the *Kerubim* with elemental air, whereas Crowley (1909/1999) associates them with elemental earth.

Angel:

פורלאך [*Forlak*]

The name is written on the Seventh Pentacle of the Sun in *The Key of Solomon the King* (Mathers (Ed.), trans. 1889/2009) and identified as belonging to an elemental angel. The etymology of the word is unclear, although the Ciceros (2006) have written, "the root of this word is *phor*, which indicates that which appears or bursts forth" (p. 136). The given English transliteration does not otherwise reveal any additional insights into its etymology or pronunciation.

Elemental king:
Gob

The source language and pronunciation of the elemental king names are unknown, as Lévi (trans. 1896/2001) never stated them. Most magicians I know who want to Rose Cross it transliterate it as גב [/gob/; n. pit or den] (see Strong, 1982b, #1358) or גוב [/guːb/; v. to dig or husbandman] (see #1461), which render words reflective of elemental earth. Crowley (1909/1999) spells the name "Ghob."

Air

Divine name:
יהוה [*YHWH* (/jĕ.hoˈwɔː/); LORD]

This is the proper four-letter name of the God of Israel (Strong, 1982b, #3068). In Jewish traditions it is ineffable – ʾ*Adonay* is spoken in place of it. The true pronunciation has been lost for quite some time (discussed in DuQuette, 2001; Kohler, 1906a; Toy & Blau, 1906). In many texts, including this workbook, the Tetragrammaton consonants are accompanied by the ʾ*Adonay* vowels. The Tetragrammaton is the *Qabalistic* divine name associated with elemental air (Crowley, 1909/1999).

Angel:
רפאל [*Rafaʾel* (/rɔː.pɔːˈʔel/); healing of god]

The name is a combination of רפא [/rɔːˈpɔːʔ/; v. to heal] (see Strong, 1982b, #7495) and אל [/ʔel/; n. god] (see #410). Though not named in *The Bible*, *Rafaʾel* is identified as an angel or archangel in various apocryphal (e.g., *Tobit*) and pseudepigraphal texts (e.g., *The Books of Adam and Eve, Books of Enoch...*). *Rafaʾel* rules over the corner of the world associated with elemental air (Agrippa, trans. 1531-1533/2004) and is the archangel of elemental air (Crowley, 1909/1999).

Angelic choirs:

אראלים [*Er'elim* (/ ʔɛr.ʔel'ɪim/)]

The root of the word is unknown in the Hebrew and Greek languages of *The Bible* (see Blau & Kohler, 1906), but it may be derived from אראל [/ ʔɛr'ʔel/; n. valiant one] (See Strong, 1982b, #691. They are not identified as choirs of angels in *The Bible*, but are in various other texts (cited in Blau & Kohler, 1906).

The name אראל [*Aral*] is the elemental angel of fire identified on the Seventh Pentacle of the Sun in *The Key of Solomon the King* (Mathers (Ed.), trans. 1889/2009) while אריאל [*Ariel*] is identified as the ruler of elemental fire (p. 74). The names אריאל [*Ariel*] and אראל [*Aral*] appear to be swapped, as the other elemental rulers listed are singular angelic choirs. *Aral* is an alternate Romanization of *Erel*, the singular form of the choirs collectively known as אראלים [*Aralim* or *Erelim*]. To further complicate things, in Agrippa (trans. 1531-1533/2004) אריאל [*Ariel*] is identified as the ruler of elemental earth (p. 257), and in *777 Revised* (Crowley, 1909/1999) אריאל [*Ariel*] is identified as the ruler of elemental air, while אראל [*Erel*] is the angel of elemental fire (p. 16).

Angel:

חסן [*Ḥasan*]

The name is written on the Seventh Pentacle of the Sun in *The Key of Solomon the King* (Mathers (Ed.), trans. 1889/2009) and identified as belonging to an elemental angel. The root of the word is unclear, but the given English transliteration suggests many candidate etymologies. It strongly resembles חסן [/ ħɔːˈsɑn̠/; v. to compact or hoard] (see Strong, 1982b, #2630) and חסן [/ ħɔ̃ˈsɑn̠/; v. possess] (see #2631). It somewhat resembles חסן [/ ħoˈsɛn̠/; n. riches, strength, or treasure] (see #2633) and חסן [/ ħɔːˈsɔn̠/; adj. strong] (see #2634).

Elemental king:
Paralda

The source language and pronunciation of the elemental king names are unknown, as Lévi (trans. 1896/2001) never stated them. The source language is probably not Hebrew or its cognate languages, as phonetic spellings render no words reflective of elemental air. Most magicians I know who want to Rose Cross it transliterate it as פרלדה, a phonetic spelling yielding *gemaṭria* values reflective of elemental air. Crowley (1909/1999) also spells the name "Paralda."

Water

Divine name:
אל [*El* (/ʔel/); god]

El may be used to refer to any deity (Strong, 1982b, #410), and is qualified with additional descriptors to distinguish *YHWH* from other gods. It is the *Qabalistic* divine name associated with elemental water (Crowley, 1909/1999).

Archangel:
גבריאל [*Gavri'el* (/gab.riˈʔel/); man of god]

The name is a combination of גבר [/gɛˈbɛr/; n. man] (see Strong, 1982b, #1397) and אל [/ʔel/; n. god] (see #410). *Gavri'el* is named in *The Bible* (Luke 1:19, *King James Bible*) and is identified as an archangel in various pseudepigraphal texts (e.g., *The Books of Adam and Eve, Books of Enoch...*). *Gavri'el* rules over the corner of the world associated with elemental water (Agrippa, trans. 1531-1533/2004) and is the archangel of elemental water (Crowley, 1909/1999).

In Jewish literature he is made of fire and is the "Prince of Fire" in all but one passage, where he is the "Prince of Water" instead (discussed in Schechter, Blau, & Hirsch,

1906). Thus, in some traditions *Gavri'el* and *Mika'el* are swapped. He frequently works with *Mika'el* to carry out the will of *YHWH*, and has been written about extensively (see Schechter, Blau, & Hirsch, 1906).

Angelic choirs:
תרשישים [*Tarshishim* (/ tɑr.ʃiʃˈiim/)]

The misspelled name is written on the Seventh Pentacle of the Sun in *The Key of Solomon the King* (Mathers (Ed.), trans. 1889/2009) and identified as belonging to an elemental angel. The name is likely from תרשיש [*Tarshish* (/ tɑrˈʃiʃ/)], a port on the Mediterranean (see Strong, 1982b, #8659). Jonah's unsuccessful attempt to flee *YHWH* by boarding a ship heading there resulted in his whale swallowing fiasco (Jonah 1:3-17, *King James Bible*). A less likely etymological possibility is its homophone for an unidentified type of precious stone (Singer & Seligsohn, 1906) incorporated in the priestly breastplate (see Jastrow et al., 1906). They are not identified as choirs of angels in *The Bible*, but are in various other texts (cited in Blau & Kohler, 1906). They rule elemental water (Agrippa, trans. 1531-1533/2004; Crowley, 1909/1999).

Angel:
טליהד [*Taliahad*]

The hyphenated name is written on the Seventh Pentacle of the Sun in *The Key of Solomon the King* (Mathers (Ed.), trans. 1889/2009) and identified as belonging to an elemental angel. The root of the word is unclear, but the given English transliteration suggests some candidate etymologies. The first part of the name strongly resembles טל [/ ʈal/; n. dew] (see Strong, 1982b, #2919). The last part of the name strongly resembles יהד [/jɔːˈhaḍ/; v. become Jewish] (see #3054).

Elemental king:
Nicksa

The source language and pronunciation of the elemental king names are unknown, as Lévi (trans. 1896/2001) never stated them. Most magicians I know who want to Rose Cross it transliterate it as נכסה because it incorporates כסה [/kɔːˈsɔː/; v. conceal or cover] (see Strong, 1982b, #3680), which renders a word reflective of elemental water. Crowley (1909/1999) spells the name "Niksa."

Fire

Divine name:
אלהים [*Elohim* (/ʔɛ̆.loˈhiim/); gods]

Elohim may be used to refer to any deities (Strong, 1982b, #430), and is qualified with additional descriptors to distinguish *YHWH* from other gods. It is the *Qabalistic* divine name associated with elemental fire (Crowley, 1909/1999).

Archangel:
מיכאל [*Mika'el* (/mɪi.kɔːˈʔel/); Who is like god?]

The name is a combination of מי [/mɪi/; n. who?] (see Strong, 1982b, #4310), כי [/kɪi/; conj. because] (see #3588), and אל [/ʔel/; n. god] (see #410). *Mika'el* is named in *The Bible* (Jude 1:9, Revelation 12:7, *King James Bible*) and is identified as an archangel in various pseudepigraphal texts (e.g., *The Books of Adam and Eve, Books of Enoch...*). *Mika'el* rules over the corner of the world associated with elemental fire (Agrippa, trans. 1531-1533/2004) and is the archangel of elemental fire (Crowley, 1909/1999).

In Jewish literature he is made of snow and is the "Prince of Water" in all but one passage, where he is the "Prince of Fire" instead (discussed in Schechter, Blau, & Hirsch, 1906). Thus, in some traditions *Gavri'el* and *Mika'el* are swapped. He frequently works with *Gavri'el* to carry out the will of *YHWH*, and has been written about extensively (see Jacobs, Seligsohn, & Montgomery, 1906; Schechter, Blau, & Hirsch, 1906).

Angelic choirs:

שרפים [*Serafim* (/ɬɔ:.rap'ıı̯m/)]

The singular name is written on the Seventh Pentacle of the Sun in *The Key of Solomon the King* (Mathers (Ed.), trans. 1889/2009) and identified as belonging to an elemental ruler. The root of the word is likely שרפ [/ɬɔ:'rɑp/; v. burning] (Strong, 1982b, #8313). In *The Bible* they flew around *YHWH* in Isaiah's vision, and touched Isaiah's mouth with a burning coal to remove his wickedness (Isaiah 6:1-13, *King James Bible*). They are not identified as choirs of angels in *The Bible*, but are in various pseudepigraphal texts (e.g., *The Books of Adam and Eve*, *Books of Enoch*...). Another etymological possibility is שרפ [/ɬɔ:'rɔ:p/; n. serpent], which is derived from the same root (see Strong, 1982b, #8314), as serpents held religious significance in the ancient world (discussed in Hirsch & Benzinger, 1906). They rule elemental fire (Agrippa, trans. 1531-1533/2004; Crowley, 1909/1999).

Angel:

אריאל ['Ari'el (/ʔɑ̃.rıı̯'ʔel/); lion of god]

The name is a combination of ארי [/ʔɑ̃'rıı̯/; n. lion] (see Strong, 1982b, #738) and אל [/ʔel/; n. god] (see #410). As the name of an angel the earliest source is unclear, however it does appear in Agrippa (trans. 1531-1533/2004), where he writes, "*Ariel* is the name of an angel, and is the same as the Lion of God; sometimes it is also the name of an evil demon, and of a city which is thence called Ariopolis, where the idol *Ariel* was worshipped" (p. 553). *'Ari'el* is also a poetic name for Jerusalem (Isaiah 29:1-2, 7, *King James Bible*).

The name אראל [*Aral*] is the elemental angel of fire identified on the Seventh Pentacle of the Sun in *The Key of Solomon the King* (Mathers (Ed.), trans. 1889/2009) while אריאל [*Ariel*] is identified as the ruler of elemental fire (p. 74). The names אריאל [*Ariel*] and אראל [*Aral*] appear to be swapped, as the other elemental rulers listed are singular angelic choirs. *Aral* is an alternate Romanization of *Erel*, the singular form of the choirs collectively known as אראלים [*Aralim* or *Erelim*]. To further complicate things, in Agrippa (trans. 1531-1533/2004) אריאל [*Ariel*] is identified as the ruler of elemental earth (p. 257), and in *777 Revised* (Crowley, 1909/1999) אריאל [*Ariel*] is identified as the ruler of elemental air, while אראל [*Erel*] is the angel of elemental fire (p. 16).

Elemental king:
Djîn

The source language and pronunciation of the elemental king names are unknown, as Lévi (trans. 1896/2001) never stated them. In Islam *djinn* are sentient beings born of fire and created before man (55:15, *The Koran*). Most magicians I know who want to Rose Cross it transliterate it as דין [/ djin/; v. judge] (see Strong, 1982b, #1778), which renders a word reflective of elemental fire. Crowley (1909/1999) spells the name "Djin."

Appendix C
Elemental Rites - Author Notes

This work was part of a larger elemental magic project that took about two years to complete. Magical diary excerpts from each rite in this workbook are as follows. Identifying information has been omitted.

Chapter 2: Earth Buries

I spent five months working with the earth element in order to be thorough. This included researching, writing, and performing everything. Progress was slow but steady.

Attuning with Elemental Earth:
I performed the attunement on and off in the same location for one month. The effect was stronger when performed multiple days in a row. You may bury yourself in dirt if you are in a location where this is possible. To include an earth tool or charm, treat it as a physical extension of your body. Physically feel the earth element vibrations pulsating into your tool or charm, empowering it. An edited excerpt from my magical diary regarding this exercise is shown in Chapter 1.

Earth Entrance Rite:
It took about 45 minutes to perform the rite. The next day Gob directed my attention towards a particular item that has been my primary elemental earth tool ever since. Also, over the next month I collected five stones when passing through various locations. They correspond to earth of earth, air of earth, water of earth, fire of earth, and aether of earth. They inspired the earth invocation and banishing rites.

Earth Element Invocation:
Excess elemental earth makes the atmosphere inside the circle thicker and heavier. The interior may also seem more inert.

Earth Element Banishing:
With banishing rites you typically don't feel anything. This rite is no exception.

Earth Element Monasticism:
I performed the Extreme Observances for 10 days. Most of my magic focused on wealth, personal transformation, and death/rebirth. One of my mundane goals during this time was to change my perspective on wealth and develop a long-term financial plan. The earth element provided some much-needed insight. I became debt free a few months after completing the monasticism. I don't think it would have happened without it.

Regarding personal transformation and death/rebirth, the earth element was helpful in making me more grounded. Many stress-related health problems were reduced or eliminated entirely. I also amplified some melancholic virtues and toned down some vices to a more manageable level.

Chapter 3: Air Carries

I spent two months working with the air element. This included researching, writing, and performing everything. I revised or completely rewrote many rites because they were composed in a hurry or on a whim.

Attuning with Elemental Air:
I performed the attunement on and off in various locations for two weeks. When I feel super light and can't hold in a ditzy, high-pitched giggle I know it worked. An incense or essential oil that gives off an odor you associate with

elemental air may also be incorporated. To include an air tool or charm, visualize elemental air particles flowing into it and empowering it.

Air Entrance Rite:
Choose a place as high as you can stand that will not bring on fear gnosis. Two days after performing the rite, my friends dragged me to a festival. There, I purchased my primary elemental air tool. It inspired the air invocation and banishing rites.

Air Element Invocation:
Attuning beforehand is recommended but not required. I typically visualize elemental air particles as tiny, luminous sky-blue dots that randomly dart around.

Air Element Banishing:
With banishing rites you typically don't feel anything. This rite is no exception.

Air Element Monasticism:
I performed the Greater Observances for six days, and then the Extreme Observances for six days immediately after. Everything that could possibly go wrong with travel or communication did. Phones, computers, air conditioners, and other devices broke. There were major phone, mail, and vehicle problems every day. People lost items more than usual, myself included. Also, the random dead birds throughout the monasticism were totally gross. On the fourth day a bird dive-bombed into my truck, busting the headlight. I didn't know that was even possible.

Ironically, most of my magic focused on communicating more effectively, being more open-minded, and improving my observation skills. At least air has a sense of humor… ALISHON MELECKTEN. The carnival of dead birds stopped abruptly after I concluded the monasticism.

Chapter 4: Water Churns

I spent three months working with the water element. This included researching, writing, and performing everything. Periods of intense activity were followed by lulls where I spent time reflecting and emotionally processing things.

Attuning with Elemental Water:
I performed the attunement on and off in various locations for two weeks. The time to attune varied greatly, probably due to location and mood. You may completely submerge yourself underwater if you are in a location where this is possible. When the attunement is successful your intuition will let you know. After attuning I feel more receptive and have less trouble receiving intuitive messages. Sometimes I also have water-related dreams that night. To include a water tool or charm, astrally sense elemental water flowing into it, empowering it.

Water Entrance Rite:
It took about 30 minutes to perform the rite. I used a bathtub with the coolest water I could stand. The colder the water, the easier it is for vibrations to manifest and be retained. Vibrating the divine names underwater is... different. Nicksa was cranky... I couldn't tell if the water was too warm for him, he was pissed off that I evoked him into a bathtub, or both. You may alter the last two lines of the Nicksa evocation if you already have an elemental water tool you feel strongly about and want to continue using – ask him to bless it instead.

Water Element Invocation:
I intuitively decided to incorporate *cakras* in the water invoking and banishing rites. After invoking I typically feel hypersensitive and extremely receptive. It is also much easier to receive intuitive messages. On the flip side I am

"out of it" for a bit afterwards because I am more in tune with the astral plane than the physical one. Other people who tested this invocation experienced similar results.

Water Element Banishing:
If you examine the invoking and banishing pentagrams banishing water is invoking air and banishing air is invoking water. In this rite you are tipping the scales towards "head" instead of "heart." This could explain why I feel more rational after banishing elemental water. Or, maybe it's just a coincidence.

Water Element Monasticism:
I performed the Extreme Observances for four weeks. Overall the monasticism was an emotional rollercoaster, as the bulk of my magic focused on unburying and dealing with subconscious rubbish. I also managed to reduce some of my biggest water vices to a less horrible level.

I had many elemental water dreams throughout the monasticism. Many friends (who had no idea what I was up to) called me to tell me about their dreams. Some of them were remarkably similar to mine. The astral form of my water tool also frequently appeared in my dreams. Doing water rites while lucid dreaming is a lot of fun!

Chapter 5: Fire Burns

I spent two months working with the fire element. This included researching, writing, and performing everything. My enthusiasm never waned, but my productivity level was inconsistent because over-eagerness led me to take on too much at once in the beginning.

Attuning with Elemental Fire:
I performed this multiple times per day for one week. The effect was stronger when performed in an environment

that was already hot. To include a fire tool or charm, treat it as a physical extension of your body. Visualize the elemental fire radiating into your tool or charm, empowering it.

Fire Entrance Rite:
It took about five minutes to perform the rite. I completed it in my living room with a large, red candle and a habanero pepper. The gnosis was intense and quick. The Djîn evocation was also fast. Afterwards, I felt warm and did not need my sweater for the remainder of the day. I'm cold natured, so that rarely happens.

During the evocation I had an intense vision of my elemental fire tool. It reflects my True Will in a personal way. Since performing the rite I feel more passionate and focused on my True Will. The fire element is what inspired me to write this workbook!

Fire Element Invocation:
This typically takes less than five minutes to perform. Afterwards I feel like I drank a cup of coffee. I also typically feel warm and energetic, and sometimes it is hard to sit still. Invoking too much elemental fire leaves me overly ambitious, scattered, and unable to focus.

Fire Element Banishing:
Sometimes I feel tired and unmotivated afterwards but am not sure if it is due to the rite or if it is just a coincidence. This rite is also useful for calming down when I am angry or panicked. I'm not sure if the effect is due to the rite, or if it's just the placebo effect at work.

Fire Element Monasticism:
I performed the Extreme Observances for five days. The time went by fast. Most of my magic focused on illumination, purification, and protection. I also did a fair

amount of cursing. This ranged from pop-culture inspired fire rites written in Klingon (a language used in the *Star Trek* series) to linking targets to cat toys and then letting my cats go nuts.

I had many elemental fire dreams throughout the monasticism. In many I interacted with various egregores affiliated with elemental fire, and sometimes I interacted with elemental fire directly. In some dreams I got yelled at for being a vindictive bitch that can't let go of things. In a few dreams I also performed impromptu fire element rites.

Chapter 6: The Elements Together

The following rites relate to the elements but were developed at different times throughout the overall work.

Elemental Balancing:
This rite may be personalized by including additional visualizations or gestures. Another option is writing a litany to each element and reciting them when you arrive the appropriate quarter. Astrally, I typically hear the sounds of happy children laughing in the east, heavy silence in the north, a woman humming or singing in the west, and battle cries in the south. In the center I typically hear white noise.

Love and Strife:
Performing a Bornless One or equivalent rite beforehand is optional. When channeling strife I extracted unwanted junk from the heads, hearts, and *cakras* of each "self." When channeling love I harmonized energies, sealed gaps, and unblocked *cakras* in each "self." Afterwards I felt more balanced and unified. Others reported similar results. You may optionally anchor this state of "perfect elemental harmony" to a word, gesture, or something else. This rite is also doable in a group as a guided meditation.

Baba Yaga Chicken Dance:
This was originally a group rite and has been performed multiple times. I consistently sigilize "courage" on my receptive hand and "cowardice" on my projective hand. Over the last few months I have been consistently less terrified driving over high bridges. I don't completely freak out... I only slightly freak out. I am also consistently less terrified of big dogs that bark a lot. Other participants had better results, perhaps because they were more specific with their traits.

Chapter 7: Aether

I spent four months working with the aether element. This included researching, writing, and performing everything. I also reflected on aether in between work with other elements.

Attuning with Aether:
I performed the attunement daily for one week with a tuning fork. The effect was stronger when performed in a still, quiet place that makes the sound vibrations easier to detect. It is useful to track the number of rings it takes for your senses to completely harmonize. The more regularly you attune, the fewer rings it will take. I typically count the number of rings on a string of prayer beads – this makes it easier to devote complete attention to the exercise without worry of losing count. If you are having trouble, feel free to alter the procedure so additional senses are more slowly incorporated.

Aether Entrance Rite:
It took about 15 minutes to perform the rite. The gnosis and overall experience focused on vibrations. Layers of observable reality were stripped back, leaving only the vibratory "essence" of what I could perceive through the senses. Different objects emitted and absorbed different vibrations. I perceived *Metatron* as a vibration underlying all the other vibrations.

Invoking Active Spirit: A Pathworking:
This was originally a group rite and has been performed multiple times. If you are short on time it is possible to abbreviate the pathworking by visiting only one or two of the elemental doors. The descriptions of the archangels are adapted from Jewish literature. The messages people receive from the archangels tend to be highly personal and bear connection to the aspect of daily life the element reigns over.

Invoking Passive Spirit: Wholehearted Surrender:
This has been successfully performed in a small group to promote friendship and unity among members. I have been working with these guys for years, so was not hesitant about being unresistingly open to our "group consciousness." Whatever the intent, the experience tends to be mentally and emotionally intense. It may take a few days or much longer to fully integrate the energy of choice.

Also, if you have to go shopping after drawing a bunch of passive banishing pentagrams you become resistant to advertising and high-pressure sales tactics.

Aether Element Monasticism:
I performed the Greater Observances for five days and then the Extreme Observances for five days immediately after. At the beginning of the monasticism I felt scattered and disjointed – my inner elements were having trouble working together. My magical diary from this time looks like a train wreck. At the end I felt much more harmonized and unified. Most of my magic focused on elemental balance, integration, and harmony.

Chapter 8: Buddhist Elements

I spent four months working with the Buddhist elements. This included researching, writing, and performing everything. It seemed like the next logical step, as they bear more similarity to the western elements than the *wŭxíng*.

Earth: Stūpa Meditation:
I performed the meditation daily for one month. Each aggregate plays an important role in the human body. Repeating the meditation reveals additional areas of the physical body where each aggregate may be found, and also exposes any elemental imbalances.

Water: Sand Maṇḍala Creation:
Bringing the sand together to create a *maṇḍala* is reflective of elemental water's cohesiveness. Overall, this is good practice for maintaining a single-pointed consciousness for a long period of time. I designed a *maṇḍala* to facilitate internal and external elemental balance. If you cannot pour the sand into naturally occurring running water let the grains disperse in the wind instead.

Fire: Expanding Awareness:
I typically feel purified and balanced after performing this meditation. The effect was more pronounced when I performed it each morning for a period of one week. Some aggregates/elements are more challenging to purify than others, but everyone is different. Others who performed this meditation reported similar results.

Air: Prayer Flag Creation:
I spent about $20 at a craft store buying squares of cloth fabric, string, and different colored paint pens. It is cheaper to buy larger pieces of cloth and then cut the squares yourself at home. This was enough for a flag with 25 cloth pieces (five of each color) cut into 30cm squares. This activity can take anywhere from a couple of hours to a weekend if you want to get really elaborate. This activity is also kid tested and approved!

Space: **Vairocana** *Invocation:*
The "Mantra of Light" may optionally be incorporated. It is *OM AMOGHA VAIROCANA MAHĀMUDRĀ MAṆI PADMA JVĀLA PRAVARTTAYA HŪṂ* [San. Praise be to the flawless, all-pervasive illumination of the great *mudrā*. Turn over to me the jewel, lotus, and radiant light (Unno, 2004, p. 1)].

Chapter 9: Chinese *Wŭxíng* [Five Phases]

I spent three months working with the *wŭxíng*. This included researching, writing, and performing everything. My approach differed from the western and Buddhist elements because the cosmology underlying the *wŭxíng* differs.

Wood: Evocation of the Azure Dragon:
I used cedar wood incense and a small picture of the Azure Dragon that easily fits in my wallet. The "horn, neck, root, room, heart, tail, winnowing basket" line is a reference to the seven star clusters in the Azure Dragon constellation. I have felt more compassionate and self-aware over the last few weeks. So far, it has stuck over the long term.

Fire: Lucky Red Paper Lanterns:
Undecorated paper lanterns can be found in major craft stores or at online retailers such as Amazon. It took about 25 minutes to perform the rite in its entirety. I originally hung my small, circular lantern in my entryway, but then moved it to the patio. In the following months I received some unexpected money, and also avoided a couple of wrecks. Otherwise, it's been pretty quiet and nothing particularly bad has happened. I have the intuitive feeling that I've avoided a bunch of misfortune.

Earth: Balancing the Phases:
This rite was inspired by a set of *wŭxíng* candles my mom bought me. I place or light each one when I call a quarter

guardian and pick up or pinch out the flame after thanking the guardian. The overall rite has a balancing, refreshing effect, and I typically repeat it whenever I'm feeling unbalanced. Though the overall rite yields decent results, I still don't think it's optimized so have continued to change it.

Metal: Evocation of the White Tiger:
I used whatever incense I had lying around and a small picture of the White Tiger that easily fits in my wallet. My friend who also tested this rite used a necklace with a metal tiger instead. The "Legs, bond, stomach, mane, net, turtle beak, three stars" line is a reference to the seven star clusters in the White Tiger constellation. Overall, I am more consistently conscious of my actions. My friend who independently performed the rite reported similar results.

Water: Ancestor Veneration:
If you are adopted and don't know much about your blood relatives or if the ones you do know about suck, focus on your positive, respectable ancestors during the rite, even if it is only one or two people.

In many traditions, salt should be avoided in the food you are offering because it is a preservative. It is said that preservatives will repel ghosts and evil spirits. If you know of a food or beverage an ancestor liked in life, feel free to include it among your offerings. In addition to my generic offering of fruits, veggies, and small candies, I offered potato pancakes to my late grandfather. I also offered him some tobacco because he was a smoker.

Other options for banishing include party poppers or a cap gun. Party poppers are frequently sold at Dollar Stores. Cap guns can sometimes be found there as well.

Chapter 10: Creating Your Own Elemental Rites
The following group rites relate to the elements but were developed at different times throughout the overall work.

Serafim *Disco Inferno:*
This rite was inspired when I saw habanero peppers on sale at the grocery store. It worked fairly well. An edited excerpt from my magical diary regarding it is shown in Chapter 1.

Lucky Charms:
I spent about $20 at a craft store buying small wooden disks, string, colorful beads, and colored paint pens. This was enough for around 40 people to each have a disk painted with their marshmallow shape. The string with decorative beads permitted everyone to wear their charm or hang it up somewhere. The more participants the merrier!

The General Mills, Inc. egregore is a "wheat Nazi" according to the volunteer that invoked. Lucky the Leprechaun's temperament did not strike us as similar to the descriptions of classical leprechauns – he just wanted to enchant the charms and cereal so he could be dismissed. Before this iteration of the rite he would try to escape, hence the chanting and the flogging. A few people reported successful "Lucky Charm" results a few weeks later.

Gaṇeśa *Stomp:*
This rite was inspired by a *Gaṇeśa* figurine my friend gave me before he moved back to India. The rite is cathartic, if nothing else. Results varied among participants, though everyone eventually overcame some of the personal obstacles they wrote down on the cards. The illumination received from the *Gaṇeśa* invocation was also deemed an important part of the process.

Appendix D

The Lesser Banishing Ritual of the Pentagram

The Lesser Banishing Ritual of the Pentagram (LBRP) is a staple in the western esoteric tradition. I have seen it used by ceremonial magicians, witches, and family tradition practitioners alike. It is a useful prelude to other magical work – it clears your working area of unnecessary junk and invokes the elemental archangels. Think of it as the magical equivalent of taking a shower or brushing your teeth every morning.

Structure

The framework for the Golden Dawn's LBRP first appears in the *Cipher Manuscripts* (Weschke, 1986), but it has been widely speculated some components have an earlier origin, as hinted at in the work of Lévi (trans. 1896/2001, pp. 63-70, pp. 237-241). Today many versions of the LBRP exist, and magicians from a diversity of backgrounds and preparations have modified it to their liking. Regardless of version the LBRP can be subdivided into three sections, discussed sequentially below.

Qabalistic *Cross:*
The magician creates a *Tree of Life* within his or her body by performing a modified version of the Sign of the Cross while saying a modified version of the last lines of the *Lord's Prayer* (see Kohler, 1906b). It may be embellished with visualizations, such as a glowing cross superimposed

on the body. The words can be spoken or vibrated. The word אמן [Heb. 'Amen; So be it!] has a rich history – see Ginzberg (1906) for details.

Drawing Pentagrams:

Drawing any sort of pentagram inherently involves working with elemental forces. The magician clears psychological and environmental junk by drawing banishing earth pentagrams in each cardinal direction while vibrating Hebrew words of power associated with *YHWH*. In many western ceremonial models earth contains the other three elements and is associated with *Malkut*. The word אהיה [Heb. 'Eheyeh; I am] is part of 'Eheyeh 'Asher 'Eheyeh [I am that I am], the burning bush's response to Moses (Exodus 3:14, *King James Bible*). The *noṭariqon* אגלא (AGLA) stands for 'Ata Gibor Le 'olam 'Adonay [You are mighty forever, (my) Lord], the first four words of the second benediction in *Shemoneh 'Esreh* (see Sossnitz & Kohler, 1906). See Appendix B for an explanation of the other verbiage.

Archangel Invocation:

The magician declares the presence of the four elemental archangels, with one located in each cardinal direction and visualized as appropriate. The verbiage in the LBRP is remarkably similar to a Jewish nighttime prayer from *The Hirsch Siddur* (1969/1982), which reads: "In the name of God, the God of Yisrael: may Michael be at my right hand, Gabriel at my left, Uriel before me, Raphael behind me, and above my head, the Presence of God" (p. 727).

Procedure

A modified version of the rite presented in the Golden Dawn's "First Knowledge Lecture" (Regardie, 1989, pp. 50-59) is as follows. If you do not have a dagger, use your finger to draw the cross and pentagrams instead. Pronunciation is conveyed in International Phonetic Association format (2015), and is based on current understanding of Biblical Hebrew phonology (Kahn (Ed.), 2013).

Qabalistic *Cross:*

1. Face east, holding your dagger in your projective hand.
2. Touch it to your head and say, אתה [ˈAta (/ʔaˈt̪ɒː/); you are].
3. Touch it to your chest and say, מלכות [Malkut (/malˈkuːt̪/); the kingdom].
4. Touch it to your right shoulder and say, וגבורה [Ugebura (/u.ɡě.buːˈrɔː/); and strength].
5. Touch it to your left shoulder and say, וגדולה [Ugedula (/u.ɡě.d̪uːˈlɔː/); and greatness].
6. Clasp your hands in front of you and say, לעולם [Le ˈolam (/lě.ʕoˈlɔːm/); forever].
7. Point your dagger up and say, אמן [ˈAmen (/ʔɔːˈmen/); So be it!].

Pentagram Drawing:

1. Draw a banishing earth pentagram in front of you and vibrate, יהוה [YHWH (/jě.hoˈwɔː/)].
2. Draw a quarter circle towards the south.
3. Draw a banishing earth pentagram in the south and vibrate, אדני [ˈAdonay (/ʔǎ.d̪oˈnɒiː/)].
4. Draw a quarter circle towards the west.
5. Draw a banishing earth pentagram towards the west and vibrate, אהיה [ˈEheyeh (/ʔɔ.hɔːˈjɔː/)].
6. Draw a quarter circle towards the north.
7. Draw a banishing earth pentagram in the north and vibrate, אגלא [AGLA].
8. Draw a quarter circle back to the east to complete it.

Archangel Invocation:
Stand with your arms outstretched to form a cross. Visualize the four archangels standing in their respective cardinal directions while saying,

> **Before me רפאל** [*Rafa'el* (/rɔː.pɔːˈʔel/)],
> **behind me גבריאל** [*Gavri'el* (/gɑb.riˈʔel/)],
> **at my right hand מיכאל** [*Mika'el* (/miɪ.kɔːˈʔel/)],
> **at my left hand אוריאל** [*'Uri'el* (/ʔuː.riˈʔel/)].
> **Before me flames the pentagram;**
> **behind me shines the six-rayed star.**

Perform the *Qabalistic* Cross one more time.

Additional Notes

Even though banishing is typically done in a counterclockwise direction, the LBRP has you move clockwise because you are invoking the archangels. Feel free to modify the rite to your liking or substitute your own. As long as it is technically sound and internally consistent with whatever system you are using, you can use anything from *Talmud* denizens to Teletubbies and it will work.

References

Aëtius (trans. 2011). In P. Curd (Ed.), *A Presocratics Reader: Selected Fragments and Testimonia* (2nd ed.). (R. D. McKirahan and P. Curd, Trans.). Indianapolis, IN: Hackett Publishing Company.

Agrippa, H.C. (2004). In D. Tyson (Ed.), *Three Books of Occult Philosophy* (J. Freake, Trans.). St. Paul, MN: Llewellyn Publications. (Original work published 1531-1533)

Alexander, P. H., Kutsko, J. F., Ernest, J. D., Decker-Lucke, S., & Petersen, D. L. (Eds.). (1999). *The SBL Handbook of Style: For Ancient Near Eastern, Biblical, and Early Christian Studies.* Peabody, MA: Hendrickson Publishers.

Altman, N. (2009). *Palmistry: The Universal Guide.* New York, NY: Sterling.

Apocalypse of Moses (trans. 1913). (R. H. Charles, Trans.). Oxford, England: The Clarendon Press.

Arikha, N. (2007). *Passions and Tempers: A History of the Humours.* New York, NY: Ecco.

Aristotle (trans. 2001). *De Caelo* [On the Heavens] (J. L. Stocks, Trans.). In R. McKeon (Ed.), *The Basic Works of Aristotle* (pp. 398-466). New York, NY: The Modern Library.

Aristotle (trans. 2001). *De Generatione et Corruptione* [On Generation and Corruption] (H. H. Joachim, Trans.). In R. McKeon (Ed.), *The Basic Works of Aristotle* (pp. 470-531). New York, NY: The Modern Library.

Aristotle (trans. 2001). *Metaphysica* [Metaphysics] (W. D. Ross, Trans.). In R. McKeon (Ed.), *The Basic Works of*

Aristotle (pp. 681-926). New York, NY: The Modern Library.

Ashcroft-Nowicki, D., & Brennan, J. H. (2001). *Magical Use of Thought Forms: A Proven System of Mental & Spiritual Empowerment*. St. Paul, MN: Llewellyn Publications.

Bardon, F. (trans. 2001). *Initiation into Hermetics* (G. Hanswille & F. Gallo, Trans.). Salt Lake City, UT: Merkur Publishing. (Original work published 1956)

Barrett, S. (2011, January 12). Be wary of acupuncture, Qigong, and "Chinese medicine." Available from https://www.quackwatch.org/01QuackeryRelatedTopics/acu.html

Bates, R. (2007). *All About Chinese Dragons*. Beijing, China: China History Press.

Beer, R. (2003). *The Handbook of Tibetan Buddhist Symbols*. Chicago, IL: Serindia Publications.

Bhattacharyya, B. (1980). *An Introduction to Buddhist Esoterism*. Delhi, India: Motilal Banarsidass.

Bhikkhu, T. (Trans.). (1997). *Dhatu-vibhanga Sutta: An Analysis of the Properties* (MN 140). Available from http://www.accesstoinsight.org/tipitaka/mn/mn.140.than.html

Bhikkhu, T. (Trans.). (2003). *Maha-hatthipadopama Sutta: The Great Elephant Footprint Simile* (MN 28). Available from http://www.accesstoinsight.org/tipitaka/mn/mn.028.than.html

Bhikkhu, T. (Trans.). (2011). *Pansu Suttas: Dust* (SN 56.102-113). Available from http://www.accesstoinsight.org/tipitaka/sn/sn56/sn56.102-113.than.html

Blake, C. F. (2011). *Burning Money: The Material Spirit of the Chinese Lifeworld*. Honolulu, HI: University of Hawai'i Press.

Blau, L., & Kohler, K. (1906). Angelology. In *The Jewish Encyclopedia* (Vol. 1, pp. 583-597). Available from http://www.jewishencyclopedia.com/articles/1521-angelology

Bodine, W. R. (Ed.). (1992). *Linguistics and Biblical Hebrew.* Winona Lake, IN: Eisenbrauns.

Brahma Net Sutra. (trans. 2000). (Sutra Translation Committee of the United States and Canada, Trans.). Available from http://www.ymba.org/books/brahma-net-sutra-moral-code-bodhisattva/brahma-net-sutra

Bryant, B. (2003). *The Wheel of Time Sand Mandala: Visual scripture of Tibetan Buddhism.* Ithaca, NY: Snow Lion Publications.

Buckland, R. (2004). *The Fortune-telling Book: The Encyclopedia of Divination and Soothsaying.* Canton, MI: Visible Ink Press.

Carrick, P. (2001). *Medical Ethics in the Ancient World.* Washington, DC: Georgetown University Press.

Carroll, P. J. (1987). *Liber Null & Psychonaut: An Introduction to Chaos Magic.* York Beach, ME: Weiser Books.

Carroll, P. J. (1992). *Liber Kaos.* York Beach, ME: Weiser Books.

Cattell, H. E. P. (2004). The Sixteen Personality Factor (16PF) Questionnaire. In M. Hersen (Ed.), *Comprehensive Handbook of Psychological Assessment* (Vol. 2, pp. 39-49). Hilsenroth, M. J., Segal, D. L. (Eds.). Hoboken, NJ: John Wiley & Sons.

Chen, C-Y. (1996). *Early Chinese Work in Natural Science: A Reexamination of the Physics of Motion, Acoustics, Astronomy and Scientific Thoughts.* Hong Kong: Hong Kong University Press.

Cherubim, D. (2004). *The Hands of Musick.* Available from http://davidcherubim.net/yod.htm

Chāndogya Upaniṣad. (trans. 1996). In *Upaniṣads* (P. Olivelle, Trans.). Oxford, England: Oxford University Press.

Chin, A. (2007). *Confucius: A Life of Thought and Politics.* New Haven, CT: Yale University Press.

Cicero, C., & Cicero, S.T. (2006). *Tarot Talismans: Invoke the Angels of the Tarot.* St. Paul, MN: Llewellyn Publications.

Codrington, R. H. (1891). *The Melanesians: Studies in Their Anthropology and Folklore.* Oxford, England: The Clarendon Press.

Confucius, (Eno, R., Trans.). (2015). *The Analects of Confucius: An Online Teaching Translation* [PDF, ver. 2.2]. Available from http://www.indiana.edu/~p374 Analects _of_Confucius_(Eno-2015).pdf

Conway, D. J. (2005). *Elemental Magick: Meditations, Exercises, Spells, and Rituals to Help you Connect with Nature.* Franklin Lakes, NJ: New Page Books.

Copenhaver, B. P. (Trans.). (1995). *Hermetica: The Greek Corpus Hermeticum and the Latin Asclepius in a New English Translation, with Notes and Introduction.* Cambridge, United Kingdom: Cambridge University Press.

Crowley, A. (1999). *777 Revised.* In I. Regardie (Ed.), *777 and other Qabalistic Writings of Aleister Crowley.* York Beach, ME: Weiser Books. (Original work published 1909)

Crowley, A. (2004). *The Book of Thoth (Egyptian Tarot).* York Beach, ME: Weiser Books. (Original work published 1944)

Cullen, F. (2006). *Vaudeville Old & New: An Encyclopedia of Variety Performers in America* (Vol. 1, pp. 952-956). Abingdon, United Kingdom: Routledge.

Dalai Lama. (2011, September 24). Reincarnation. Available from http://www.dalailama.com/messages/ statement-of-his-holiness-the-fourteenth-dalai-lama- tenzin -gyatso-on-the-issue-of-his-reincarnation

Demerath, N. J., III (2003). *Crossing the Gods: Worldly Religions and Worldly Politics*. New Brunswick, NJ: Rutgers University Press.

DuQuette, L.M. (2001). *The Chicken Qabalah of Rabbi Lamed Ben Clifford*. York Beach, ME: Weiser Books.

Ede, A. (2006). *The Chemical Element: A Historical Perspective*. Westport, CT: Greenwood Press.

Eliot, T. S. (2009). *On Poetry and Poets*. New York, NY: Farrar, Straus and Giroux. (Original work published 1943)

Eysenck, H. (1998). *Dimensions of Personality*. New Brunswick, NJ: Transaction Publishers. (Original work published 1947)

Feng, G., & Du, Z. (2015). *Traditional Chinese Rites and Rituals* (J. Huang & Y. Jiang, Trans.). Newcastle, United Kingdom: Cambridge Scholars Publishing.

Flowers, S.E. (Ed.). (1995). *Hermetic Magic: The Postmodern Magical Papyrus of Abaris*. York Beach, ME: Weiser Books.

Fludd, R. (1659). *Mosaical Philosophy*. London, England: Humphrey Moseley.

Fortune, D. (2000). *The Mystical Qabalah* (Rev. ed.). York Beach, ME: Weiser Books. (Original work published 1935)

Ginzberg, L. (1906). Amen. In *The Jewish Encyclopedia* (Vol. 1, pp. 491-492). Available from http://www.jewish encyclopedia.com/articles/1383-amen

Gouin, M. (2010). *Tibetan Rituals of Death: Buddhist Funerary Practices*. Abingdon, United Kingdom: Routledge.

Greene, L. (1978). *Relating: An Astrological Guide to Living with Others on a Small Planet*. York Beach, ME: Weiser Books.

Grimes, J. A. (1995). *Ganapati: Song of the Self*. Albany, New York: State University of New York Press.

Hall, M. P. (1928). *The Secret Teachings of all Ages: An Encyclopedic Outline of Masonic, Hermetic, Qabbalistic and Rosicrucian Symbolical Philosophy.* Available from http:// www.sacred-texts.com/eso/sta/

Hill, L. (2013). *Blood: A Biography of the Stuff of Life.* Toronto, ON: House of Anansi Press.

Hippolytus (trans. 2011). *Refutation of All Heresies.* In P. Curd (Ed.), *A Presocratics Reader: Selected Fragments and Testimonia* (2nd ed.). (R. D. McKirahan and P. Curd, Trans.). Indianapolis, IN: Hackett Publishing Company.

Hirsch, E., & Benzinger, I. (1906). Seraphim. In *The Jewish Encyclopedia* (Vol. 11, pp. 201-202). Available from http://www.jewishencyclopedia.com/articles/ 13437-seraphim

Hirsch, E. G., Muss-Arnolt, W., McCurdy, J. F., & Ginzberg, L. (1906). Cherub. In *The Jewish Encyclopedia* (Vol. 4, pp. 13-16). Available from http://www.jewish encyclopedia. com/articles/4311-cherub

Hirsch, S. R. (1982). *The Hirsch Siddur.* Nanuet, NY: Feldheim Publishers. (Original work published 1969)

Hoffman, J. F. (2004). *In the Beginning: A Short History of the Hebrew Language.* New York, NY: New York University Press.

International Phonetic Association. (2015). IPA Chart. Available from https://www.internationalphonetic association .org/content/full-ipa-chart

Jacobs, J., Seligsohn, M., & Montgomery, M. W. (1906). Michael. In *The Jewish Encyclopedia* (Vol. 8, pp. 535-538). Available from http://www.jewishencyclopedia.com/ articles/10779-michael

Jacobs, J., & Blau, L. (1906). Metatron. In *The Jewish Encyclopedia* (Vol. 8, p. 519). Available from http:// www.jewishencyclopedia.com/articles/10736-metatron

Jastrow, M. et al. (1906). Breastplate of the High Priest. In *The Jewish Encyclopedia* (Vol. 3, pp. 366-367). Available from http://www.jewishencyclopedia.com/articles/ 3668-breastplate-of-the-high-priest

Jouanna, J., & van der Eijk, P. (Ed.). (2012). *Greek Medicine from Hippocrates to Galen: Selected Papers* (N. Allies, Trans.). Leiden, The Netherlands: Brill.

Kahn, G. (Ed.). (2013). *Encyclopedia of Hebrew Language and Linguistics* (Vol. 3, P-Z). Leiden, The Netherlands: Brill.

Kaplan, A. (Trans.) (1997). *Sefer Yetzirah: The Book of Creation in Theory and Practice* (Rev. ed.). York Beach, ME: Weiser Books.

Kenton, R. (n.d.). A Qabalistic View of the Chakras. Available from http://www.kabbalahsociety .org/wp/articles/a-kabbalistic-view-of-the-chakras/

Kern, M. (2009). Bronze Inscriptions, the Shijing and the Shangshu: The evolution of the ancestral sacrifice during the western Zhou. In J. Lagerwey & M. Kalinowski (Eds.), *Early Chinese Religion, Part One: Shang Through Han (1250 BC – 220 AD)* (pp. 143-200). Leiden, The Netherlands: Brill.

Khalsa, S. (1998). *Kundalini Yoga: The Flow of Eternal Power.* New York, NY: Perigee.

King James Bible (1611). Available from http://www.king jamesbibleonline.org

Kohler, K. (1906a). Adonai. In *The Jewish Encyclopedia* (Vol. 1, pp. 201-203). Available from http://www.jewish encyclopedia.com/articles/840-adonai

Kohler, K. (1906b). Lord's Prayer, The. In *The Jewish Encyclopedia* (Vol. 8, pp. 183-184). Available from http://www.jewishencyclopedia.com/articles/10112-lord-s-prayer-the

The Koran (trans. 1993). (J. M. Rodwell, Trans.). New York, NY: Ballantine Books.

Krishnaswami, U. (1996). *The Broken Tusk: Stories of the Hindu God Ganesha*. Little Rock, AR: August House.

Kumar, R. (Ed.). (2003). *Essays on Indian Art and Architecture*. New Delhi, India: Discovery Publishing House.

Leadbeater, C. W. (2005). *The Astral Plane: Its Scenery, Inhabitants and Phenomena*. New York, NY: Cosimo Classics. (Original work published 1895)

Lerner, L. S. (1996). *Modern Physics for Scientists and Engineers* (Vol. 2). Sudbury, MA: Jones and Bartlett Publishers.

Lévi, E. (trans. 2000). *The Great Secret, or, Occultism Unveiled*. York Beach, ME: Samuel Weiser, Inc. (Original work published 1898)

Lévi, E. (trans. 2001). *Transcendental Magic: Its Doctrine and Ritual* (A. E. Waite, Trans.). York Beach, ME: Weiser Books. (Original work published 1896)

Levitt, S. (1998). The Five Taoist Elements: Fire, earth, metal, water and wood. *Feng Shui* 4(1): pp. 22-25.

Lindahl, J. R. (2010). The Ritual Veneration of Mongolia's Mountains. In J. I. Cabezon (Ed.), *Tibetan Ritual* (pp. 225-248). Oxford, United Kingdom: Oxford University Press.

Maciocia, G. (2015). *The Foundations of Chinese Medicine: A Comprehensive Text* (3rd ed.). Publisher: Elsevier.

Magini, L. (2015). *Stars, Myths and Rituals in Etruscan Rome*. Publisher: Springer International. doi:10.1007/978-3-319-07266-1

Marshall, A. (2006). Shamanism in Contemporary Taiwan. In J. Miller (Ed.), *Chinese Religions in Contemporary Societies* (pp. 123-146). Santa Barbara, CA: ABC-CLIO.

Mathers, S. L. (Ed.). (2009). *The Key of Solomon the King* (Mathers, S. L., Trans.). Mineola, NY: Dover Publications. (Original work published 1889)

McClelland, N. C. (2010). *Encyclopedia of Reincarnation and Karma.* Jefferson, NC: McFarland & Company, Inc.

Michelson, A. A., & Morley, E. W. (1887). On the Relative Motion of the Earth and the Luminiferous Ether. *The American Journal of Science, 34*(203), pp. 333-345.

Miles, J., & Hempel, S. (2004). The Eysenck Personality Scales: The Eysenck Personality Questionnaire Revised (EPQ-R) and the Eysenck Personality Profiler (EPP). In M. Hersen (Ed.), *Comprehensive Handbook of Psychological Assessment* (Vol. 2, pp. 99-107). M. J. Hilsenroth, D. L. Segal (Eds.). Hoboken, NJ: John Wiley & Sons.

Mistlberger, P. T. (2010). *The Three Dangerous Magi: Osho, Gurdjieff, Crowley.* Winchester, United Kingdom: O-Books.

National Center for Complementary and Integrative Health. (2017, March 23). Traditional Chinese medicine: In depth. Available from https://nccih.nih.gov/ health/ whatiscam/chinesemed.htm

Novella, S. (2012, January 25). What is Traditional Chinese Medicine? Available from https://sciencebased medicine.org/what-is-traditional-chinese-medicine

Page, T. E. et al. (Eds.) (trans. 1959a). *Nature of Man* (W. H. S. Jones, Trans.). In T. E. Page et al. (Eds.), *Hippocrates: Vol. IV* (pp. 1-42). Cambridge, MA: Harvard University Press. (Original work published 1931)

Page, T. E. et al. (Eds.). (trans. 1959b). *Humours* (W. H. S. Jones, Trans.). In T. E. Page et al. (Eds.), *Hippocrates: Vol. IV* (pp. 61-96). Cambridge, MA: Harvard University Press. (Original work published 1931)

Page, T. E. et al. (Eds.). (trans. 1959c). *Regimen I* (W. H. S. Jones, Trans.). In T. E. Page et al. (Eds.), *Hippocrates: Vol. IV* (pp. 223-296). Cambridge, MA: Harvard University Press. (Original work published 1931)

Page, T. E. et al. (Eds.). (trans. 1959d). *Regimen in Health* (W. H. S. Jones, Trans.). In T. E. Page et al. (Eds.), *Hippocrates: Vol. IV* (pp. 45-59). Cambridge, MA: Harvard University Press. (Original work published 1931)

Page, T. E. et al. (Eds.). (trans. 1959e). *Aphorisms* (W. H. S. Jones, Trans.). In T. E. Page et al. (Eds.), *Hippocrates: Vol. IV* (pp. 97-221). Cambridge, MA: Harvard University Press. (Original work published 1931)

Paracelsus (trans. 1996). *Liber de Nymphis, Sylphis, Pygmaeis et Salamandris et de Caeteris Spiritibus* [A book on nymphs, sylphs, pygmies, and salamanders, and on the other spirits] (Trans. H. E. Sigerist). In H. E. Sigerist (Ed.), *Four treatises of Theophrastus von Hohenheim, called Paracelsus: Translated from the original German, with introductory essays* (pp. 213-254). Baltimore, MD: The Johns Hopkins University Press.

Parfitt, W. (1991). *The New Living Qabalah: A Practical & Experimental Guide to Understanding the Tree of Life.* Boston, MA: Element Books.

Pausanias (trans. 1918). *Description of Greece.* In *The Perseus Catalog.* Available from http://www.perseus.tufts.edu /hopper/text?doc=urn:cts:greekLit:tlg0525.tlg001.perseus -eng1:10.24.1

Pepin, M. (1989). The tree in Yetzirah. *The Kabbalist.* Available from http://internationalorderof kabbalists.org /Public/Kabbalist%20Articles/Kabbalist%201989/The%2 0Tree%20in%20Yetzirah%20-%20Pepin%20(1989).pdf

Perkins, D. (2013). *Encyclopedia of China: The Essential Reference to China, its History and Culture.* New York, NY: Routledge. (Original work published 1999)

Plato (n.d.). *Timaeus* (Trans. B. Jowett). *The Internet Classics Archive*. Available from http://classics.mit.edu/Plato /timaeus.html

Plutarch (trans. 2011). *On the E at Delphi*. In P. Curd (Ed.), *A Presocratics Reader: Selected Fragments and Testimonia* (2nd ed.). (R. D. McKirahan and P. Curd, Trans.). Indianapolis, IN: Hackett Publishing Company.

Raleigh, A. S. (1993). *Hermetic Science of Motion and Number*. Publisher: Health Research Books. (Original work published 1924)

Regardie, I. (1989). *The Golden Dawn* (6th rev. ed.). Woodbury, MN: Llewellyn Publications.

Rehmus, E. E. (1990). *The Magician's Dictionary: An Apocalyptic Cyclopaedia of Advanced Magic(k)al Arts and Alternate Meanings*. Port Townsend, WA: Feral House.

Reid, S. (1996). As I do will, so mote it be: Magic as metaphor in neo-pagan witchcraft. In J. R. Lewis (Ed.), *Magical Religion and Modern Witchcraft* (pp. 141-168). Albany, NY: State University of New York Press.

Rinpoche, Z. (n.d.). The Meaning of om mani peme hum. Available from http://www.abuddhistlibrary.com/ Buddhism/A%20-%20Tibetan%20Buddhism/Authors/ Za%20Choeje%20Rinpoche/The%20Meaning%20of%20O m%20Mani%20Peme%20Hum/The%20Meaning%20Of% 20Om%20Mani%20Peme%20Hum.htm

Samten, L. (n.d.). Tibetan sand mandalas. Available from http://www.losangsamten.com/mandalas.html/

Sangharakshita. (1996). *Tibetan Buddhism: An Introduction*. Birmingham, United Kingdom: Windhorse Publications.

Schechter, S., Blau, L., & Hirsch, E. G. (1906). Gabriel. In *The Jewish Encyclopedia* (Vol. 5, pp. 540-543). Available from http://www.jewishencyclopedia.com/articles/6450-gabriel

Schmiechen, M. (2009). Newton's Principia and Related 'Principles' Revisited: Classical dynamics reconstructed in the spirits of Goethe, Euler and Einstein. In *Elementary and Local Mechanics* (Vol. 2, 2nd ed.). Berlin, Germany: Herstellung und Verlag: Books on Demand.

Schwartzman, S. (1994). *The Words of Mathematics: An Etymological Dictionary of Mathematical Terms Used in English.* Publisher: Mathematical Association of America.

Scott, J. L. (2007). *For Gods, Ghosts and Ancestors: The Chinese Tradition of Paper Offerings.* Hong Kong: Hong Kong University Press.

Selin, H. (Ed.). (1997). *Encyclopaedia of the History of Science, Technology, and Medicine in Non-Western Culture.* Publisher: Springer-Science+Business Media, B. V. doi: 10.1007/978-94-017-1416-7

Shapiro, F. R. (Ed.). (2006). *The Yale Book of Quotations.* New Haven, CT: Yale University Press.

Shingon Buddhist International Institute. (1998/1999). The Teaching of the Six Great-elements. Available from http://www.shingon.org/teachings/ShingonMikkyo/rokudai.html

Simonyi, K. (2012). *A Cultural History of Physics* (D. Kramer, Trans.). Boca Raton, FL: CRC Press. (Original work published 1978)

Simplicius (trans. 2011). *Commentary on Aristotle's Physics.* In P. Curd (Ed.), *A Presocratics reader: Selected fragments and testimonia* (2nd ed.). (R. D. McKirahan and P. Curd, Trans.). Indianapolis, IN: Hackett Publishing Company.

Simpson, J. (2012). *The Book of Angelic Elements* [PDF]. Publisher: Archan Publishing.

Singer, I., & Blau, L. (1906). Uriel. In *The Jewish Encyclopedia* (Vol. 12, p. 383). Available from http://www.jewish

encyclopedia.com/articles/14606-uriel

Singer, I., & Seligsohn, M. (1906). Tarshish. In *The Jewish Encyclopedia* (Vol. 12, p. 65). Available from http://www. jewishencyclopedia.com/articles/14254-tarshish

Skilton, A. (2001). *A Concise History of Buddhism*. Birmingham, United Kingdom: Windhorse Publications. (Original work published 1994)

Smith, W. (1862). *A New Classical Dictionary of Greek and Roman Biography, Mythology and Geography, Partly Based upon the Dictionary of Greek and Roman Biography and Mythology*. C. Anthon (Ed.). New York, NY: Harper & Brothers.

Sossnitz, J., & Kohler, K. (1906). AGLA. In *The Jewish Encyclopedia* (Vol. 1, p. 235). Available from http://www. jewishencyclopedia.com/articles/899-agla

Starhawk (1999). *The Spiral Dance: A Rebirth of the Ancient Religion of the Great Goddess* (20th anniversary ed.). New York, NY: HarperSanFrancisco. (Original work published 1979)

Stein, R. L., & Stein, P. L. (2016). *The Anthropology of Religion, Magic, and Witchcraft* (3rd ed.). New York, NY: Routledge.

Strausbourg Papyrus, *ensemble* a. In P. Curd (Ed.), *A Presocratics Reader: Selected Fragments and Testimonia* (2nd ed.). (R. D. McKirahan and P. Curd, Trans.). Indianapolis, IN: Hackett Publishing Company.

Strong, J. (1982a). Greek Dictionary of the New Testament. In *Strong's Exhaustive Concordance of the Bible*. Nashville, TN: Broadman & Holman.

Strong, J. (1982b). Hebrew and Chaldee Dictionary. In *Strong's Exhaustive Concordance of the Bible*. Nashville, TN: Broadman & Holman.

Thera, Ñ., & Bodhi, B, (Trans.). (1994). *Maha-sihanada Sutta: The Great Discourse on the Lion's Roar* (MN 12). Available from http://www.accesstoinsight.org/tipitaka /mn/mn. 012.ntbb.html

Thurman, R. A. F. (Trans.). (1994). *The Tibetan Book of the Dead: Liberation Through Understanding the In Between.* New York, NY: Bantam Books.

Tibi, S. (2006). *The Medicinal Use of Opium in Ninth-Century Baghdad.* Leiden, The Netherlands: Brill.

Toy, C. H., & Blau, L. (1906). Tetragrammaton. In *The Jewish Encyclopedia* (Vol. 12, pp. 118-120). Available from http://www.jewishencyclopedia.com/articles/14346-tetragrammaton

Trainor, K. (2004). *Buddhism: The Illustrated Guide.* Oxford, United Kingdom: Oxford University Press.

Trainor, K. (2006). *Relics, Ritual and Representation in Buddhism: Rematerializing the Sri Lanka Theravada Tradition.* Cambridge, United Kingdom: Cambridge University Press.

Tzu, L. (trans. 1989). *The Complete Tao Te Ching* (Trans. G. F. Feng & J. English). New York, NY: Vintage Books.

Unno, M. (2004). *Shingon Refractions: Myōe and the Mantra of Light.* Somerville, MA: Wisdom Publications.

Wang, A. (2000). *Cosmology and Political Culture in Early China.* Cambridge, United Kingdom: Cambridge University Press.

Wen, B. (2016). *The Tao of Craft: Fu Talismans and Casting Sigils in the Eastern Esoteric Tradition.* Berkeley, CA: North Atlantic Books.

Weschcke, C. L. (1986). Foreword and Appreciation. In *The Golden Dawn* (6th rev. ed., pp. ix-x). Woodbury, MN: Llewellyn Publications.

Wetzel, J. S. (2001). *The Paradigmal Pirate*. Publisher: Author.

Whittick, A. (1960). *Symbols, Signs and Their Meaning*. London, United Kingdom: Leonard Hill.

Williams, P., Tribe, A., & Wynne, A. (2012). *Buddhist Thought: A Complete Introduction to the Indian Tradition* (2nd ed.). Abingdon, United Kingdom: Routledge. (Original work published 2000)

Wolfe, A. (1998). *Elemental Power: Celtic Faerie Craft & Druidic Magic*. St. Paul, MN: Llewellyn Publications.

Wong, E. et al. (Trans.). (2012). *Celebrate Chinese Culture: Chinese Auspicious Culture* (Wong, E., L. L. Cheng, C. S. Boon, W. S. Ee, & J. Chong, Trans.). Singapore: ASIAPAC Books under authority of Beijing Foreign Language Press.

Wood, E., & Subrahmanyam, S. V. (Trans). (1911). *The Garuda Purana* (Abridged ver.). Available from http://sacred-texts.com/hin/gpu/index.htm

Wynn-Jones, V. (2015, November 4). Elemental Correspondences. *Pagan News 2.0*. Retrieved November 11, 2016 from http://www.pagannews.com/wp/2015/11/04/the-elements-and-their-correspondences/

Xuan, W. (2011). Traditional Chinese Medicine: An overview. In C.-S. Yuan, E. J. Bieber, & B. A. Bauer (Eds.), *Traditional Chinese Medicine* (pp. 97-112). Boca Raton, FL: CRC Press.

Young, I. (Ed.). (2003). *Biblical Hebrew: Studies in Chronology and Typology*. London, United Kingdom: T & T Clark International.

Yuqun, L. (2011). *Traditional Chinese Medicine*. Cambridge, United Kingdom: Cambridge University Press.

About the Author

Soror Velchanes is a practicing chaos magician and avid paradigm surfer living in Scottsdale, Arizona. She grew up practicing various forms of magic with family and friends, and now enjoys teaching her nephews the art and science of magic. She has been an active member of the Illuminates of Thanateros since 2003, and occasionally teaches classes on chaos magic, pop culture magic, and more, in the Greater Phoenix area. She has also been a Certified Professional Tarot Reader since 2005.

Learn more about her published works at
http://www.velchanes.com

Recent Titles from Megalithica Books

Zodiac of the Gods by Eden Crane

A new interpretation of the Egyptian Dendera Zodiac, this book explores character analysis for each sign, revealing your relationship with the deity presiding over your month of birth. The book also offers a primer for Egyptian magic, focusing upon the deities of the year. The vivid pathworkings enable you to connect with these ancient gods and goddesses, and work with their energy to influence and improve your life, helping you realise your goals and desires. ISBN: 978-1-912241-03-3 Price: £11.99, $16.50

The Heart of the Elder by Lillith ThreeFeathers & Joy Wedmedyk

Elders are a vital component of pagan and neopagan traditions. This book offers all you need to know about them. Learn how to identify, meet, and work with Elders and the distinguishing characteristics of great Elders. This book teaches how to originate and maintain meaningful relationships with your Elders and unique teaching styles. It illumines the mysterious benefits of training with Elders and includes amazing stories of life-changing events. ISBN: 978-1-912241-04-0 Price: £9.99, $12.99

Reiki Subversives Manual by Karl Hernesson

Introducing a radical new approach to energy healing. Become a Reiki warrior and urban healer to heal yourself, your community and the Earth – even if you're not attuned to Reiki. This book includes a basic method for using Earth energy, as well as a process to connect to Reiki, so you can begin urban healing yourself. Heal your environment and connect with the healing power of the planet. ISBN: 978-0-9932371-3-3 Price: £11.99, $16.50

www.immanion-press.com

Egyptian-Themed Magic
From Megalithica Books
www.immanion-press.com

Sekhem Heka by Storm Constantine

Drawing upon her experiences in Egyptian Magic and the energy healing systems of Reiki and Seichim, Storm Constantine developed this new system to appeal to practitioners of both magic and energy healing. Incorporating ritual and visualisation into a progressive journey through the seven energy centres of the body, Sekhem Heka can be practiced by those who are already attuned to an energy healing modality, as well as those who are simply interested in the magical aspects of the system. Sekhem Heka is designed to help the practitioner work upon self-evolution and self-knowledge. Each of the seven tiers focuses upon a particular Ancient Egyptian god or goddess, including practical exercises and rites. ISBN pbk: 9781905713134, $21.99, £12.99

Graeco-Egyptian Magic by Tony Mierzwicki

Graeco-Egyptian Magick outlines a daily practice involving planetary Hermeticism, drawn from original texts and converted into a format that fits easily into the modern magician's practice. Graeco-Egyptian magick represents the last flowering of paganism before it was wiped out by Christianity. It blends ancient Sumerian and Egyptian magick with the relatively more modern Greek and Judaic systems. It includes a recreation of a planetary system of self-initiation using authentic Graeco-Egyptian practices from the first five centuries C.E. This is a practical intermediate level text aimed at those who are serious about their spiritual development and already have grounding in basic spirituality, but beginners who carefully follow the instructions sequentially should not be deterred. ISBN pbk: 1905713037, $21.99, £12.99

The Travellers' Guide to the Duat by Kiya Nicoll

Planning a trip to the Egyptian spirit world? Like any responsible traveller, you want to know something about the history, geography, and politics of your destination. You want to know what documents you need to have in order for customs and immigration, what precautions to take, how to book a boat tour, where to stay, what to eat, and when you'll get the most interesting sightseeing opportunities. Laced through its humorous presentation you will find extensive information about ancient Egyptian religion and magical practice. Renditions of ancient spells in modern poetry mark each section, showing the ancient magical texts in a new light. The Beautiful West awaits! Book your tour today! ISBN pbk: 9781905713738, $19.99, £10.99

CPSIA information can be obtained
at www.ICGtesting.com
Printed in the USA
LVHW091311120121
676293LV00008B/12